I Screwed Up! Now What?

7 Practices to Make Things Right — and to Conquer Adversity

Josh Bacon, Ph.D.

WALNUT STREET BOOKS

LANCASTER, PENNSYLVANIA

walnutstreetbooks.com

D1310911

Cover and page design by Cliff Snyder and Mike Bond

I Screwed Up! Now What?

Copyright © 2022 by Josh Bacon

Photo Credits

Photo of author on page 256 by Jon Styer.

Paperback: 9781947597501
PDF, EPUB, and Kindle: 9781947597518

Library of Congress Control Number: Data available.

I Screwed Up! Now What? is published by
Walnut Street Books, Lancaster, Pennsylvania

info@walnutstreetbooks.com

"Fate whispers to the warrior,
'You cannot withstand the storm.'
The warrior whispers back, 'I am the storm.'"

I Screwed Up! Now What?

To my three daughters: Emma, Maya, and Tessa.

I know storms and failure will come to you. My hope

is that you will use every one of them to make things

right and grow into the person God intended you to be.

Take the challenge, take the risk, for each of you is

"the storm."

Contents

Part 2: *The Restorative Practices Journal*

An Introduction to Part of My Story

◆◆◆

I first met Malieka when she walked into my office with her head hung low, saying she wanted to drop out of college. As Dean of Students, I was responsible for helping students with the drop-out process.

She took a second to compose herself and then looked up. She said this was her dream school. She wanted to graduate and become a nurse to help people, but she couldn't take it anymore and just wanted to go home.

At this point in my career I had been meeting with students for over 20 years, and Malieka, like many students before her, had a story to tell. I had learned that there always seemed to be an initial reason a student was withdrawing, but, with time, a deeper reason usually emerged. It was important to create the environment and space where students could share their stories and their authentic selves.

I told Malieka I could help her withdraw from the university, but first, could she tell me what was going on? Malieka, a sophomore, said she was failing most of her courses and felt like she didn't belong here anymore.

I continued to listen. Malieka started to share more and more about why she wanted to leave and why she felt her grades were so bad this semester. She said she had always dreamed of becoming a nurse and came here to fulfill that dream. But the classes were too hard and she wasn't smart enough. Malieka kept saying, "I don't belong here," and "I can't handle the workload." She finally burst into tears and said, "I'm just a complete failure."

I offered Malieka a box of tissues and continued to listen. I asked her why she felt like a failure.

"Everyone else here is doing so well. It seems so easy for them. They get good grades and party at the same time. I can't handle it all. I have to work a part-time job and I just can't do it anymore."

Why a Restorative Group?

Malieka was already on academic probation and had been assigned to meet with a Restorative Group once a week. The first meeting of the group was scheduled for the next week. I told her more about the group and that we would all be working together, sharing our stories.

Malieka said she didn't have any time to meet with a group, she was too busy, and she just wanted to go home. At that moment she received a call from her father. She said she had to take it and stepped out of the office.

When she came back about five minutes later, she handed me her phone. "My dad wants to talk to you. I'm so sorry."

I took Malieka's phone. "Hi, this is Dean Bacon." After a few minutes of conversation, I thanked her father, urged him to stay in touch, and asked him to call me if I could help with anything in the future.

Malieka said, "I told my father I would give it another month and try this group process with you."

Over the years of meeting with so many students who were dropping out of college, I heard "I don't belong here" and "I am a failure" hundreds of times. I knew from experience there was always more to the story. I had learned to be patient, to try to understand the why behind their urge to drop out. Malieka was very closed off and didn't reveal much during our first meeting. I was thankful that she was willing to give college a little more of a chance and work with our Restorative Group.

I hoped that this pilot Restorative Group would help create an environment where she could share the deeper story of why she was leaving her "dream college."

I saw Malieka the next week at our first Restorative Group meeting. She was one of 12 students who had to complete a 10-week program for those who were on academic probation but indicated they were struggling with more than academics and could use extra support.

We used Restorative Circles to build community in the group, and, as the instructor, I shared some of my stories of how I struggled in college. Students always found it hard to believe that their Dean of Students had once been on academic probation and had gotten into trouble on multiple occasions himself.

During the fourth week, the wonder of the Restorative Group took place. Something in the group changed. In the earlier three weeks the group had become comfortable with a Circle Process and working in small groups with their peers. Then, during week four's Circle check-in, we all told something that no one in the group knew about us. Students took the time to share some heavy, personal stories about themselves. They finally felt comfortable telling some of the deep harm they had experienced.

At the end of class, three students waited to talk with me. Malieka was second in line. During the sharing in our Circle Process that evening, she mentioned that her mother had passed away the prior summer, and she was not handling things well. As I talked with the first student in line, I noticed Malieka crying. The student behind her hugged her as she sobbed in her arms. When I asked Malieka what was going on, she said, "I hadn't told anyone about my mother passing away. I don't know why I shared it with the group. I was just feeling so lost and overwhelmed."

Even though I had been using Restorative Practices for over 10 years, I was amazed at what the process could do for students who were struggling. It had taken three weeks of small group Circle work, sharing activities, and challenging homework for Malieka to open up and talk about why she was struggling.

Over the years I have found there are no shortcuts to help students who are struggling. It takes working through the Seven Key Practices to help transform them and get them back on track. I had been experimenting with small Restorative Groups to help create the challenging and supportive environment necessary for students to do the hard work of overcoming their struggles and making things as right as possible. This would help them be successful in college and overcome future adversity. Malieka was finally sharing her story and being her true authentic self.

A major challenge is that every student is different. What works with one student might not work with another. Experimenting with all Seven Practices creates space to work with each person's individual needs.

As the group continued to meet, Malieka began to share the negative self-talk going on in her head since her mother passed. All 12 of the students in the Restorative Group started to tell their stories as well, becoming their authentic selves to the others. They were each coping with very personal, difficult situations, although each was unique. No wonder they were on academic probation or facing academic suspension. What still amazes me is that every one of these students was trying to function on their own, not talking about their difficulties with anyone else until the group started to meet.

What is a Restorative Process or Response?

When we talk about making things as right as possible and using a Restorative Process, it is about making meaning of the struggles we face. When you screw up, it's how you respond that makes a lasting impact on your life.

A Restorative Response means using all the tools in this book to make things as right as possible, and to also make yourself stronger and wiser so you're unlikely to make the same mistakes again. Living restoratively, and responding to adversity restoratively, is about making meaning from the setbacks in our lives and using them as ways to grow, to be accountable for our transgressions, and to rise stronger.

Throughout the semester we all expressed our stories, our struggles, and our fears. Many students opened up for the first time, a lot shed tears, and many offered a helping hand to their peers. Nearly all had deeply rooted harms in their lives and a lot of unmet needs.

Everyone in the group seemed to lack a method for addressing adversity and the setbacks in their lives. They felt they were failures or losers and didn't belong in college. They didn't realize that they had been through challenging times before and had the ability within themselves to meet the current problem, while actually becoming stronger in the process.

Not only did we help Malieka address her current struggles, but we gave her a process for addressing adversity and setbacks for the rest of her life. It was not easy, and it took time and support, but Malieka now knew that storms would come into her life, but they would not break her. She had learned the Seven Practices that would assist her in growing stronger from the storms that would come her way.

Through this Restorative Group, we challenged and supported each other, doing weekly assignments that helped us examine ourselves. Some of the students became very close, continuing to meet with each other and offer peer support after the class was over. I continued to mentor some of them long after the required number of meetings.

Part of mentoring and coaching others through *The Restorative Practices Journal* (Part 2 of this book) is to share your own journey and your own setbacks. In order to be our authentic selves and model deep sharing, we leaders also need to open ourselves up and participate in the Restorative Processes.

I have been knocked down, beaten up, and failed more times than anyone else I know—or at least it feels that way. That's an almost universal feeling. All of us experience these struggles—what I call storms—usually without telling anyone what we're going through or how we're feeling. It doesn't really matter what type of storm you face or what others think of your experience. What matters is the meaning you make of it and how you experience the recovery.

This book will help you make meaning of your setbacks and suggest how to use them to grow stronger and wiser. Or how to use your experience to mentor someone else through a storm. A resilient person is not afraid of taking risks because they've been through storms before and have discovered a way out.

But we must all be careful not to compare our definition of a storm to someone else's. Don't let anyone tell you your storm is not a storm. You may be told to get over it, or that what you're experiencing is nothing compared to what others are going through. Life is not a competition, and how we experience different setbacks varies greatly. Some of the most challenging storms people face are inside their heads where no one else can see.

Having been through many storms, I have changed my inner self-talk and my view of how the storms fit into my life story. I realize now that my failures prepared me to be a Dean of Students on a college campus and work with thousands of students who face struggles and failures. Many of these students have a negative inner dialogue going through their heads when they come to my office. They think they're failures who don't belong in college.

This book with its *Journal* is for *anyone* who has screwed up, struggled, or faced setbacks or a recent failure. It is also for anyone who is supporting or mentoring someone through a screw-up, struggle, setback, or failure.

If you're inclined to quickly hide your mistakes and failures, and don't attempt to examine them and make meaning from them, you may find this book to be helpful. The *Restorative* Process is based on over 20 years of assisting people in applying these Seven Practices to their struggles. During those 20 years I often failed, and then spent time examining those failures to learn what actually worked. I constantly asked myself what would have helped me change my habits and shake me loose from the negative self-talk and patterns I had been caught in.

Getting Unstuck

Learning Restorative Practices and discovering the value of a journal helped me a lot. In working with thousands of people of all ages, and through much trial and error, I have found Seven Key Practices that work. You can learn this process, practice these methods, and develop a Restorative Support Network. But ultimately the motivation to change is up to you.

Why "Restorative"? Restorative Practices point to an ancient way of addressing conflict, adversity, and challenging situations. Restorative Practices involve creating a space and mindset to be your authentic self. They call for humbling yourself to make things right within yourself and with your environment.

Restorative Practices are about recovery and restoration. They are action-oriented. They ask you to rediscover yourself with energy, even with fierce determination. This is how we recover from life's struggles. Not only do we recover, but we come back stronger and with more energy. Our failures and setbacks change us. I am a different person after a setback and failure. The choice is mine as to how I will let the experience affect me.

Without examining, sharing, or reflecting on our failures we often become weaker or stuck in the "I'm a failure" mindset. The Restorative Process requires the challenging work of sharing your setback story with others and examining the setback in relation to your overall life story. This Process also teaches all of us how to make meaning of the failures in our lives and how to use them as valuable learning experiences, which in the end makes us stronger and wiser.

If you're using this book to help yourself—or someone you care about—to be restored from a recent struggle in life, you will find step-by-step practices here that have been successful. Watching someone you care about go from failure to failure without changing is extremely painful.

You can do this Restorative work with a mentor or support group. Sharing is one of the Seven Practices that is key to making things right and becoming the person you say you want to be.

If you are supporting someone through this process, you will need to share your struggles, too. What you share is up to you. The key is to be your authentic self and model openness.

I do not suggest one simple thing that will change your life, or an easy mantra that will make you the person you have always wanted to be. Lasting growth doesn't work that way. From my 20 years of working with people facing struggles, I can attest that it takes deep examination of oneself, which can only be done within a Restorative environment and with support around you. I have learned how resistant to change people can be, so draw on as many parts of the processes and practices in *The Restorative Practices Journal* (beginning on page 136) as you need.

I've had more than my share of screw-ups and failures, of being unsuccessful in many endeavors I chose to pursue. I seemed to be good at nothing—I was too small, not smart enough, and had no talent. That sounds like an awful experience and a terrible way to grow up, but that wasn't the whole story. The beauty of it is I'm still here, I'm still standing, and all those falls made me stronger, wiser, and better able to help the people I serve today.

I needed years to develop this healthy perspective about my life and my struggles. While it was happening, I felt alone and scared, sure that I was doomed to a life of failure. I was sure my life was destined to be one storm after another, which led to a severe tempest of negative thoughts in my head. I internalized all my setbacks and failures. The running narrative in my head was: I'm a screw-up, I'm weak, I'm stupid, and why would anyone want to be around a person like me?

What I did not realize when it was happening was that after all those times I was knocked down, beaten up, and failed, I continually got back up, and I never quit. The storms battered me and tried me. But I see, upon reflection, they made me stronger and helped me create more durable roots so I could face bigger storms in the future.

People who have risen from adversity are not afraid to take risks or stretch themselves because they know they have been knocked down before. They know they have a process for getting back up. In the end, what matters is, "You are still here, still standing." This is the key—not *what* happens to us but how we *make sense* of what happens to us.

As most of us know, growing up can be difficult. Kids can be brutal to each other, and before all the bullying awareness programs it was even worse. In that environment I kept pushing, I kept trying new things, kept taking risks, and always tried to find a way.

When you learn to make meaning of the storms in your life, you can begin to take risks strategically, to stretch yourself, challenge yourself, and brave the furor. It took a lifetime of looking at my own story of failures, but also working with countless

---

RESTORATIVE QUESTIONS

What is your current or most recent struggle story? Write down your failure, setback, or storm. Get some paper, or enter your thoughts on your phone, tablet, or laptop.

———————————

Who are your current support people? Who do you go to because you're comfortable sharing with them when you're struggling? You might want to tell them what you've just written.

> ## RESTORATIVE QUOTES
>
> *"Who dares, wins."*
> British Special
> Air Services motto
>
> *"Just when the
> caterpillar thought
> the world was over, it
> became a butterfly."*
> Chuang Tzu

others to help them make meaning of their setbacks, to come up with a strategy and process for responding to the tornados that we each face.

Now I use my storms to grow, learn, and rise stronger and wiser. Now if I screw up, make mistakes or bad choices, or have self-doubt, I have a process that I have used and shared with others. It has changed my story and the direction of my life.

I want to share the process with you so that you can change your story from one of failure to being a fighter who can face any challenge and struggle that comes into your path. Typhoons will come. Screw-ups are inevitable if we are striving. But we've been in storms before. The fact that we are still here means they did not break us.

The Seven Practices I discovered over the years that have helped to restore me and others from our struggles and screw-ups are:

1. Sharing
2. Self-Talk
3. Restorative Practices
4. Mentoring
5. Motivation to change
6. Self-Care
7. Challenge and support

PART 1

I SCREWED UP

CHAPTER ONE

Sharing

To go fast, walk alone. To go far, walk together.

RWANDAN PROVERB

Sharing. It sounds simple, but that's what I was missing my entire young life. No one told me about their failures, and I never talked about mine. In the environment in which I grew up, sharing those kinds of stories would have been seen as a sign of weakness.

When no one is talking about failures, people believe that life for others around them is great and easy, and that everyone else is thriving. I assumed that everybody but me was doing well, and there wasn't even Facebook or Twitter back then for people to show off their perfect lives. Social media gives the impression that everyone else is successful and happy. My friends are easily navigating work, school, and relationships, and they're doing it with perfect hair and happy smiles—or so it appears.

Left alone with my failures, I created my own inner, silent story about how my life was full of mistakes. They're what made me who I am. For many years, the dominant story in my head with every setback I faced was, "You are still just a little screw-up who won't amount to anything." It was painful and I suffered.

At times I go back to those deeply seated narratives in my head that society reinforced and I chose to believe. It took me a long time—years of reflection, unlearning, and helping others rise from their setbacks—to learn a process that changed how failure fits into my life and how it can fit into yours.

I have learned to use failure and setbacks as opportunities to rise stronger and wiser. By reflecting on my past, and through sharing my setback stories with others, I have gained wisdom. I didn't realize that my deepest internal fears and self-talk would eventually help me understand the power of sharing and the power of restoring myself. The ability to grow wiser and rise stronger was always in me, and it is in you, too. You can also unlock this potential and gain this freedom.

I want to show you how to do this and help you share your own story of rising stronger. We tend to treat failure as something awful that should never be discussed. We view setbacks as unpleasant, not something to tell people about, and definitely not something to post on social media. But if you are alive, setbacks and failures are inevitable, and they will be a part of your life. They can break you down and add to your negative self-talk. Or they can help you grow and make you stronger.

> ### RESTORATIVE QUOTE
>
> *"The miracle is this: The more we share the more we have."*
>
> LEONARD NIMOY

People who achieve greatness and excellence often have screwed up more than most. If you challenge yourself and take risks, failure is more likely to occur. In fact, if you are not failing or facing struggles, you may not be challenging yourself enough.

People don't like to talk about their struggles and failure because they think it makes them appear weak. We like to talk about success, wins, promotions, and all the good stuff. It would not be much fun to post on Facebook and Twitter about a major failure that just occurred in your life. But sharing is one of the most courageous things you can do for others. Sharing our setbacks shows others that we trust them and care enough about our relationship to be vulnerable and truthful with them.

Failures and setbacks are events we can learn to be accountable for. If you listen to people or follow their social media, you would think no one ever fails. We are all walking around living our best lives and succeeding in everything we do. This culture is unhealthy, particularly for youth and young adults.

Here's what happens: when failure and setbacks inevitably come, the current culture leads people to believe they are the only ones experiencing it. Your self-talk becomes, "I'm a loser, a failure, I'm all alone in this." Feeling alone during your most challenging and weakest time is a recipe for disaster.

Left alone to think about your failure, particularly if you are young, you create your own story. One of the first things you likely think is, "I'm not normal." You compare yourself to your peers and what people post on social media. With no outside perspective to counter your inner voice, you spiral into feeling that you don't belong. That, particularly for a young adult, can put your mental health in jeopardy.

I remember my first day of college orientation. My dad drove me two and a half hours to campus. All I had was a duffle bag. We didn't say one word to each other on the drive. When we pulled up to what was to be my home for the next four years, it was crowded, and there was no place to park.

I'm not sure if it was the times, or my family dynamics, but my dad did not even get out of the car when he dropped me off. He simply said, "Why don't you just get out here?" Before I could grab my duffle bag and exit the car he added, "You know about condoms, right?" I quickly and uncomfortably mumbled, "Yes, Sir." As I exited the car and

> ### RESTORATIVE QUOTE
>
> *"It is in the shelter of each other that people live."*
>
> IRISH PROVERB

grabbed my duffle bag, he said, "Call your mother every once in a while," and he drove off.

Now that I work in higher education and have shared this story with others, I've reframed it by saying, "My dad didn't talk much, but he seemed to have a way of cutting right to the important stuff." I'm not sure how everyone else's college experience started, but that was mine.

We had no parent orientation, and my parents didn't come into the residence hall and set up my room. I spent that first day learning about the campus and signing up for classes—on my own.

During the transition to college, I remember everyone else seeming so happy and confident. My roommate must have gotten there before me, because his side of the room was decorated. He had stuff everywhere. I threw my one duffle bag on the bed and tried to settle in. At one point, when I was alone in my room and terrified, I thought, "I can't do this. I don't want to be here. Why is everyone except me so happy and excited? What's wrong with me?"

I was reinforcing the running dialogue in my head: "I'm different, a failure, and this is a huge mistake." The next five years of college would be an up and down struggle. That's right. Because of my many struggles it took me that long to graduate. My five-year undergraduate experience includes academic failure, social blunders, being arrested twice, athletic failures on the football field, and transferring schools.

Now that I work at a college, I reflect back on my experiences to help students learn from my mistakes. With perspective, I've come to realize that almost everything that happens can be put to good use. My college experiences helped prepare me to eventually work with struggling college students.

Which story to tell ourselves?

When I became Dean of Students, I researched what institutions around the country do to encourage resiliency. One theme emerged: "Sharing." All the best universities in the country have some type of program that allows struggling students to share their experiences with others. People need to tell others their stories of setbacks and failures. Many of the top Ivy League colleges and universities have created programs so that students talk about their stories of failures, often in online video formats.

Sharing often takes away the power and the weight of the failure, and it stops us from having to bear the burden alone. It exposes to the light what once was in darkness. By sharing our stories, we are creating a community of support, and we are helping others to learn from our mistakes.

College administrators often strive to create a sense of belonging at their institution. In my experience of meeting with students who have faced setbacks, I have found they often think they don't belong, that they are alone in their struggles, and that everyone else is thriving. But that's a misreading. They often conclude, "I don't belong here and I need to leave." Many colleges, in their mission statements, aspire to authentic sharing in an open community.

But our larger culture avoids talking about our failures and struggles openly with others, particularly if you have been raised with the idea that, "Failure is not an option, failure is for the weak, and setbacks do not happen to us."

These are lies. We need to create a culture where failure and setbacks are embraced as a vital part of one's learning process.

Sharing our stories in community restores our sense of self, helps us reflect on our experiences, lets us rise stronger, and leads us to true identity development, which ultimately helps us thrive. You will learn through the Restorative Process different methods and approaches for sharing your setbacks and failures.

This book would be too long if I told all of my failures and setbacks, but I am going to bring up some of them to illustrate the process I have found helpful. And I will include stories of the many college students I have worked with over the past two decades as Dean of Students at a mid-sized college on the East Coast. I have changed the students' names and identifying characteristics in these stories.

Ask someone about their most recent screw-up and see how they respond. Usually their eyes dart immediately to the floor and their head points downward. Failure is not a comfortable topic. Many college students' self-image starts with their pride in thinking, "I was accepted into the top college of my choice." Or "I was accepted into the eight universities I applied to." They do not mention the six others that did not accept them.

As an educator, I know that failure is part of the growth process, particularly in human development, and it is even more important during our younger years. Failure is one of the ways we make sense of our world. It is how we eliminate behavior that doesn't work for us. In science, failure is an important step in moving toward the outcome that finally leads to success. By eliminating what does not work and what does not lead to success, we eventually find out what does work.

Developing a lifelong Restorative approach to responding to setbacks can lead you to become the person you say you want to be and fulfill your dreams.

Before we talk about what works, let's discuss what is not helpful. Blaming others, blaming the environment, blaming circumstances, in essence, blaming anyone or anything other than yourself is often what happens. Our current culture seems obsessed with people blaming things outside their control.

RESTORATIVE QUOTE

"The unexamined life is not worth living."

SOCRATES

I encountered Eric during my first year as Dean of Students. Eric changed his major eight times. He believed that if he failed a test or struggled with a particular course, he was a failure and could not complete the program. So every time things didn't come easily, he determined he did not belong in that major and switched to another. Eric's false belief that he was a failure eventually led him to drop out of school and become a bus driver. It took many hours of sharing his setbacks and failures, and many hours of reflecting on these experiences, for Eric to come to realize that he did not have a process for responding to setbacks that would allow him to rise stronger.

Even minor setbacks in life can lead people to quit. The ability to stick with something and work through the challenges and struggles is what the Restorative Process teaches. Eric was under the false assumption that everyone else was breezing through their courses, that no one else failed their tests, and everyone except him was not only succeeding, but succeeding with ease. These are the false narratives we often develop when we live in a culture that does not share authentically.

Eric took this self-talk and developed a story about himself that said, "I'm a failure—I can't succeed in college. Being a bus driver is all I can ever be." For Eric to change that, he needed a Restorative space for him to share his story. When an open and trusting environment was created that allowed Eric to be vulnerable and share his authentic self, he was able to start the Restorative Process of examining his failures. He became aware of his negative self-talk, his lack of self-care, and the absence of a support system for himself. He had never really examined his life and how the multiple setbacks had formed his life story.

A Restorative response can engage and rescue any of us, wherever we are on our journeys. Then we are able to look honestly at how we have responded to life's setbacks and failures. We learn a new way of recognizing and responding to these critical life moments. Eric came to realize that failures and setbacks could become great opportunities to learn, grow, and rise stronger. By talking with others about his setbacks and failures, he grew toward becoming the person he said he wanted to be. Eric went on not only to graduate, but to earn a master's degree.

There are steps, practices, and methods you can learn to do this, but ultimately how you respond is up to you. There is no *one* way to rise stronger and grow from life's storms. Through practice and sharing your setbacks, you can learn the Restorative approach to rising stronger that is best for you. I encourage you to experiment, work with others, practice, and use the techniques in these chapters to develop your own personal method for responding to life's challenges.

> ### RESTORATIVE QUOTES
>
> *"My failures have been errors in judgment, not of intent."*
> ULYSSES S. GRANT
>
> *"I have learned over the years that when one's mind is made up, this diminishes fear; knowing what must be done does away with fear."*
> ROSA PARKS

I cannot think of a more important and needed skill to develop than the ability to use setbacks and failures to rise stronger and become the best version of yourself.

Among my favorite stories of leaders who continue to pick themselves up, learn from their failures, and never give up is America's eighteenth president and Union Civil War General, Ulysses S. Grant. Did you know that before the Civil War, General Grant was seen in St. Louis, wearing a tattered old military coat and selling firewood from the back of a wagon? Prior to being a general, Grant failed at many business ventures and had rock-bottom moments that left him struggling just to feed his family. Grant's last resort was to take a job in his father-in-law's business in order to provide for his wife and children. During the Civil War, General Grant was known for making bold moves against the

> ## RESTORATIVE QUESTIONS
>
> *Who are you* comfortable enough with to share your struggles and authentic self?
>
> _____
>
> *Who can mentor* you through a Restorative Process?
>
> _____
>
> *Who are some* potential participants who could form a group to work through a Restorative Process together with you? Put their names down. Add more if you think of others.

enemy. This tactic had been missing up until the time of Grant's leadership and helped turn the tide of the Civil War.

Some attribute Grant's ability to take risks and make bold moves to his earlier life struggles, having nearly bottomed out prior to the war. Grant had seen hard times and braved major storms in his life. He was able to use those experiences to restore himself and grow wiser and stronger. Grant was not afraid to take risks and stretch the Union Army. He did not run from major gales, but knew he could brave them and recover. Grant found a way to use the storms and struggles of his life to develop humility, as well as a "grind" mentality that led to winning the Civil War eventually and bringing about the end of slavery. I did not hear about Grant's struggles and his ability to grow from them until I was 50 years old. This part of his story isn't widely known. Instead, most of us have heard only about the accomplished general and U.S. president that Grant was.

J. K. Rowling, the author of the Harry Potter books, overcame her low moments and life struggles to come up with good writing, creating a tale that made a major mark on the world. Rowling said, "Failure meant a stripping away of the inessential. I stopped pretending to myself that I was anything other than what I was, and began to direct all my energy into finishing the only work that mattered to me. Had I really succeeded at anything else, I might never have found the determination to succeed in the one arena where I believed I truly belonged."

CHAPTER TWO

Self-Talk

"Limits, like fears, are an illusion."

MICHAEL JORDAN

"You yourself, as much as anyone in the entire universe, deserve your love and affection"

BUDDHA

"I failed because I'm a failure." This is the negative self-talk we need to learn how to change. It's not what happens to you that matters most; it is what you say to yourself *about* what happened that matters.

One of the things I constantly catch myself saying in my head is, "You are still just a dumb little screw-up." I have a fear of speaking in public, and, unfortunately for me, I've had to speak in public a lot. I remember in middle school, that before I had to give a "speech," I got sick each time. My good friends Lionel and Gilbert made fun of me. I laughed on the outside, but inside I felt like such a loser.

By examining this struggle over the years, I realize that I have "imposter syndrome." I often think, "Why in the world would anyone want to hear from me? Don't they know what a little dumb screw-up I was growing up?"

By looking honestly at my life, and sharing with a mentor, I now know this self-talk is deeply rooted in the way I viewed myself growing up. When I am at my most vulnerable, in front of a large crowd getting ready to speak, this negative self-talk comes back. I never told anyone about this running self-talk in my head as I was growing up, so by not sharing and examining it, I allowed it to become my identity.

Understanding self-talk

Take a minute and think about what you've said to yourself today. Was it critical? Was it judgmental? Or was it kind and helpful? How did you feel after you engaged in this inner discussion? Is this the way you would talk to someone you care about?

Your thoughts are the source of your emotions and moods. The conversations you have with yourself can be destructive or beneficial. They influence how you feel about yourself and how you respond to events in your life. Your self-talk becomes your behaviors, your behaviors become your habits, and your habits become who you are.

What is self-talk?

Self-talk is something you do naturally throughout your waking hours. Positive self-talk is a powerful tool for increasing your self-confidence and curbing your negative emotions. People who can master positive self-talk are thought to be more confident, motivated, and productive.

Although positive self-talk comes naturally to some, most people need to learn how to cultivate positive thoughts and dispel the negative ones. With practice, it can become more natural to think good thoughts rather than bad ones.

Positive self-talk

Positive self-talk is supportive and affirming. Consider the following two inner statements:

- ❖ "I'm going to speak up in the meeting today because I have something important to contribute." This sounds like a positive plan and attitude.
- ❖ "I don't think I want to speak up in the meeting today because I'll look foolish if I say the wrong thing." Compare this negative comment with the statement above.

See how these contrasting inner dialogues can change the way we engage with the world and interact with people.

Ruminating

Ruminating is the flip side of positive self-talk. It happens when you replay upsetting or cringe-worthy thoughts or events over and over again in your head. Thinking through a problem can be useful, but if you spend a lot of time ruminating, small issues tend to grow bigger. Constantly ruminating can make you more likely to experience depression or anxiety.

I grew up the shortest, skinniest kid in my class for most of my young life. In my environment and community, how tough you were and what you did as an athlete became the measurements of what kind of person you were. I had a distant father who became angry at the drop of a hat. If I showed what he thought was any sign of weakness, he let me have it. Since I was the smallest guy in this environment, I became a little screw-up. This was the self-talk and the narrative that went through my mind like a revolving video.

Any time I faced a struggle, had a setback, or failed, it was added to the narrative in my head: "Yep, you are a little screw-up." This took place alone in my head. Because I never shared it or discussed it, this thought was never challenged. Under these circumstances, I became the little punk that I thought I was.

Acting tough—Hiding scared

When I started to grow and change in appearance, it was too late. My self-identity was already there. I told myself, "You may be bigger now and doing well athletically, but you are still just a little screw-up." I learned how to fight back and be tough in order to survive, but inside I was still a scared little punk.

On the outside I learned to never back down from a fight, and I learned how to succeed in sports. I chose the toughest sport they were playing in my neighborhood: football. If social media had been around when I was growing up, I could have posted a very successful outward appearance. But I never shared my inner feelings with anybody. That would have shown weakness.

Everyone I hung out with was doing the same thing as I was. Since no one shared their setbacks and failures, I thought everyone else was doing great. They didn't seem to have the self-doubts I had. They never seemed to fail like I did. Everyone—as far as I could tell—was confident, happy, and breezing through life. Meanwhile, I felt increasingly that something was wrong with me, that I didn't belong, and that I was less than.

I went to college looking like a strong, successful athlete. I had never processed all my negative self-talk and negative identity. I was doomed before I even got started. College seemed no different from high school. Everyone else was doing great, so happy and so confident, bouncing along through life. College seemed to come easy to them.

On the outside, everyone seemed to be thriving. So why wasn't I? Without sharing my story or hearing other's stories, I came to believe that something was wrong with me and that I didn't belong there. In the absence of talking honestly about my feelings, I would distract myself and work my frustrations out on the football field.

One day during the first week of classes, I sat in my room, paralyzed, not wanting to go anywhere. I was sure that everyone would see me for the fraud that I was. I didn't belong in higher education because I wasn't smart enough. But over the years I had developed a way of getting through my negative self-talk. I could fake it, I could convince myself that I was a tough football player and that you were no better than I was. For me, that meant you may be smarter than I am, but I will kick your ass.

I was talking the talk and looking the part, but I hadn't done the hard work of examining my inner self-talk and making meaning of my screw-ups. Instead, I thought, I'm here to play football, and you're no better than I am. You're just students, but I'm an athlete, so I puffed up my chest and walked outside, looking like a strong, successful football player. That worked for a little while, and I was successful on the football field even as a first-year student.

Making space for honest talk

Looking back, I wonder how many other people were scared on the inside just like me, thinking they didn't belong. Yet all of us were unwilling to share and show any sign of weakness or vulnerability. Now that I work at a college, I know many students carry these feelings. What if we had a space where we could be our authentic selves, let down our fake outward facades, and share struggles openly? This is the space that *The Restorative Practices Journal* (see pages 136-254) and the Restorative Process create.

I survived orientation, and then very quickly football took over all of my spare time. I had no time to reflect and examine my self-talk, assess what kind of person I was becoming, where I wanted to go in life, or who I wanted to be. For me it was football. For others it may be video games, alcohol, social media, online shopping, drugs, or whatever distracts you from being your authentic self and reflecting on your innermost thoughts.

Back in the day, we started out with three-a-day football practices. They were as brutal as they sound. Today, schools are allowed to have only one practice a day with required water breaks, concussion protocols, and no-contact days. Back then, 180 kids tried out for the college football team. By the end of two weeks of three-a-days, there were 70 left. Under these conditions there was a huge need for resilience and grit. With that many players trying out for the team, coaches could afford to have a lot of people quit. In fact, they didn't have enough helmets in the beginning, so some players started without helmets. As people dropped out, they passed their helmet to the next guy.

You find out pretty quickly under such circumstances who has what it takes to play college football, and, more importantly, who has the ability to persevere and rise stronger from being knocked down and beaten up. Most guys didn't have what it took to meet the challenge. The coaches pushed us to the brink of failure, and many quit. On one particular day when it was over 100 degrees, more than 20 people quit.

I started as a tenth string fullback. There were so many of us at practice that they had to put our names on our helmets with tape, so they knew who we were. During a break in practice, all the fullbacks and running backs were sitting around, telling their statistics from high school and all the honors they had won. I hadn't won any honors in high school. In fact, I didn't play fullback in high school. I was an offensive lineman. I couldn't rattle off all the touchdowns I scored or yards I ran for like they could. Once again, I felt like a little screw-up who didn't belong. But the one thing I did have, and what I had learned growing up as that little punk, was that nobody was going to outwork me. I could take anything and keep coming back.

By this time, football was the one place I was confident, the one place where I would never back down. I would scrap and fight with anyone on the football field. Sometimes I got knocked down extremely hard, but I always got up. By the end of the season I had gone from tenth string to second string, and played on all the special teams.

Unfortunately, I never reflected on my experiences at that time and never extended resiliency on the football field to resiliency in the classroom or other areas of my life. I knew how to work hard during the football season, and I could bust my butt in the off-season to get better. But at that time, I never expanded being resilient into other parts of my life. I never found someone to share with who might have helped me think more broadly in an open and honest way. I did not have someone with experience and hard-fought wisdom to help me make meaning in all the parts of my life.

So when the first day of classes began, I was not prepared for the academic challenge. When the classroom got hard, I quit. Socially, I struggled. I coped with negative behaviors and bad habits. At this time in my life I had no mentors or role models to show me another way. What I realize now is that people were there who could have helped me, but I wasn't ready to learn. Instead, the dialogue running through my head said, "Why would anyone want to help a little punk like me?" I was literally terrified to talk to my professors and college coaches.

One day at practice, we were going over plays for the upcoming game. In football, the first and second team units go against the backup players. They call the backup players the "scout team," and they run the other team's plays on offense and defense.

I was having a bad practice. The head coach yelled at me and sent me down to be on the scout

RESTORATIVE QUESTIONS

What have you thought about yourself since your most recent failure?

———————

How respectful is your self-talk to yourself?

———————

How much forgiveness do you give yourself?

———————

Just start writing and see what answers you find within yourself.

team. I went down with the scout team or, as we called them, "the scrubs." I quickly learned that running the offense of the other team was not easy. Our defense was really good, and they would beat the hell out of the scout team. The culture on the scout team was to go easy and make the defense look good. If you deviated from that agreed-upon method, you paid for it.

After practice, as I was changing, the senior captain, whose locker was next to mine, asked me what was wrong. I told him I was mad at being moved to the scout team. He said, "You can stay mad and be like all the other scrubs and go easy day in and day out. Everyone will say 'good job, thanks for making us look good,' and you will stay with the scout team all year. Or you can play like you don't want to be there and stop trying to make us look good. Stop feeling sorry for yourself and work harder."

I respected him and I listened. For a senior captain to take an interest in a freshman—a scrub, a punk like me—was powerful. So the next day at practice I treated it like it was game day. I got my ankles taped and went through my game-day rituals. For the first play on the scout team I ran the ball and went full speed into one of our starting defensive linebackers. I knocked him down and broke into the open field.

When you're playing with a bunch of scrubs who are all going half-speed, trying not to get hurt and trying to make the defense look good, it's pretty easy to stand out. The scout team coaches saw how hard I was going and kept giving me the ball. The coaches were loving it.

The starting defense was not loving it—and it went on from there. They tried to kill me. There were fights, pushing and shoving, and a lot of hard hits. The coaches loved it, the scout team actually got excited, and we started going at it. It was an intense practice, and I left the field exhausted and bloody. When I got to the locker room, the senior captain who was on defense asked what the hell got into me. I said, "I took your advice." He said, "Good job. That's the look we need every day."

The coaches reviewed the tapes from practice every day, and after seeing how hard I played, they never put me down with the scout team again. The truth was, I wasn't doing anything that great. Everyone else on the scout team was going half-speed, and it made me look really good.

In hindsight, I was learning, practicing, and developing the habit of outworking everyone else, no matter what happened. For someone who felt they had no God-given qualities or skills, the one thing I could control and do was outwork everybody. I started to develop a reputation of being a hard worker, a tough kid.

I never shared the wisdom I learned from that experience until years later when I was a veteran player. I was amazed at how many people accepted their position on the scout team and went through a whole season at half-speed, making the defense look good. Everyone patted them on the back and said, "Good job."

I didn't realize how important that senior's advice was at the time. He took just a few moments to share it with me. He was a captain and someone I looked up to, so I listened. He showed he cared about me and my success. His advice worked, and I used it the rest of my time playing college football. Eventually I would be a veteran player, and I would pass on this advice to many freshmen.

When I became Dean of Students, I loved working with athletes and told this story to many of them over the years. Some of these life experiences became the roots of a process I developed to help many people I worked with overcome their own setbacks and challenges.

The power of self-talk

If you're a young adult and keep your self-talk inside, it will tend to become your self-identity. (The same is true for a child.) Without anyone to counter our inner dialogue, what we tell ourselves becomes a part of who we are, and we begin to believe it.

When you do not share with others, you think your perceptions are right. You look at their outward appearances and their social media images, and you think they have it together. In college, too many individuals are walking around thinking, "I'm the only one who isn't thriving here. I'm the only one who is failing. I'm the only one who's not ready." These reflections lead people to think they don't belong. I can tell you from 20 years in higher education, you are far from the only one.

My academic experience during my freshman year was a struggle. I never reflected and examined my habits, and I never learned to apply my methods on the football field to the classroom. I was in college for the wrong reasons, and I chose to be a business major. I thought maybe owning my own business one day would be cool, but I really gave it no more thought than that. Then I took accounting my freshman year. I failed accounting, and that was the end of my being a business major and my thought of one day owning my own business.

It didn't have to be the end of those dreams, but at that time in my life, when I struggled and failed in the classroom, I quit. The truth was I had no passion for owning my own business and no passion for being a business major. I had not learned to apply my work ethic in athletics to the classroom, so I was unable to persist in the classroom when things got tough. These early experiences would have a big influence when I learned more about working with young adults and Restorative Justice. I could relate to students who were struggling academically and causing trouble outside the classroom.

As Dean of Students, I was sent one of our college's women's basketball players. She was an outstanding basketball player who had earned a Division One scholarship. By all outward appearances, she was thriving. I was asked to work with her because she was struggling mentally on the court and with her classes. I saw a lot of myself in this student. She came off as extremely tough and together. It took weeks of meeting one on one, and sharing our stories, for her to finally break down and tell me the extremely negative self-talk going through her head on a daily basis. She said she had never let anyone else know about this self-talk before and was scared of what people would think of her. She eventually agreed to give counseling a try and started to do the hard work of unpacking her history and examining her self-talk.

I was amazed to learn, when she visited me several years later, about how important she thought the experience of examining her self-talk was in her life. It led her to feeling so much relief inside, so that she was better able to be her authentic self with people. She told me that she hated having to meet with me at first, and really didn't like the idea of going to counseling. But that experience was the best part of college for her and started a path to healing in her life. It is often through our struggles and failures where we learn and grow the most.

The need to examine and change your self-talk

Self-talk is a big part of who you are. The constant dialogue in our heads is how we make meaning of the events in our lives. What we constantly tell ourselves is who we become. The self-talk after a setback or failure gives the event meaning and begins to shape who we think we are, how we think of ourselves, and how we place this event into the story of our lives. It is useful to examine our self-talk particularly after a setback or failure. If you're like most people, your self-talk is likely harsh and critical. In general, it may be something like "I'm a failure," not "I failed." The difference in these two statements is extremely important. One is a label of who you think you are. The other is a temporary description of something you've experienced.

For years the dialogue in my head after something went wrong was, "See, you are a dumb little punk. I knew I couldn't do this, which this failure just proved."

Your self-talk eventually becomes what you think of yourself. Because you're telling yourself this on a daily, ongoing basis, it becomes who you are. Why are we so hard on ourselves? Why don't we give ourselves a break like we would give other people? When someone comes to you after they have failed, do you tell them they are a loser or a failure?

I was mentoring Ruth, who constantly told me she was so lucky to be in college and so lucky to have been picked to be a leader in student government. I finally said, "I have known you for over a year, and I don't think your success has anything to do with luck."

It wasn't until her graduation when she told me that my comment to her was the first time anyone ever challenged her way of thinking about herself. She said, "It helped me to think that the Dean of Students and advisor to student government sees me this way. So why can't I see myself this way?" She said she had begun to "interrupt herself" whenever she started to think that her success was luck. We may need someone else to work with us to help us examine and change our self-talk.

Examining your self-talk is a critical, lifelong practice that can lead to major changes in who you become.

Recording your self-talk

❖ Share your self-talk with the support networks you develop while going through *The Restorative Practices Journal*.

❖ Or write your self-talk in your *Journal*. Honest examination is essential to making lasting changes. Sharing is critical. We all need someone we trust to help counter our negative self-talk and put it in correct perspective.

❖ Write down the words that are in your head. Write down how you have framed a setback in your life and what you say about yourself. Be open, honest, and vulnerable. Monitoring your constant self-talk, and ultimately changing your self-talk, are skills that take practice.

❖ If you struggle with negative self-talk, you might find it helpful to see a professional counselor.

Keeping track of your self-talk and journaling what you say to yourself, including when you say it, and what is going on at the time you say it, can be helpful. Becoming aware of these self-talk patterns is the first step in developing a plan to change the ongoing dialogue in your head.

When you notice yourself starting down the path of negative self-talk, you can cut it off and learn to insert a positive affirmation phrase instead. Below is a sample of what a self-talk journal might look like. This is included in *The Restorative Practice Journal* in the second part of this book (see pages 136-254):

Date and time	Self-talk	Circumstances at the time	Reframed with encouraging affirmation

I have worked hard over the years to change my inner conversation. When something happens outside of my control, I now say to myself, "Negative to positive." This starts a thinking process for me that goes like this: "This could be a bad situation and lead to something negative. How can I flip things and turn this into an opportunity for something positive, or to make the situation even better?"

I do this a lot when it comes to my physical wellness. For example, if I'm scheduled to work out at the gym, and I show up but the gym is closed, I try to find another solution. Years ago I'd say, "Oh well, guess I can go home and sit on the couch." Now I intentionally say to myself: "Negative to positive." I look for a way to do a different workout that is even harder. What could have set me back is actually now forcing me to move forward.

When you face a struggle or fail, self-talk is how you internally start making meaning of the event. If you haven't examined and practiced being aware of your self-talk, you can easily fall back into the same old inner conversations you've used since childhood. What we say to ourselves reinforces old stories about who we are. They're usually based on fear or trauma. This negative self-talk, when unchecked, leads to the creation of a negative self-identity.

Awareness of your self-talk during a hard time is the beginning of the Restorative Process and of changing how you make meaning from the struggles you face.

> ### RESTORATIVE QUOTE
>
> *"Talk to yourself like you would to someone you love."*
>
> Karoline Kurkova

Anger and frustration

When we fail, we often become angry. Sometimes we direct that anger toward others or the circumstances. It's okay to feel angry. It means you care and that you're not happy with failure. If you aren't angry, it means you're okay with failure.

Your anger, when angled in the right direction, is powerful in helping you learn and grow from this setback. It can lead to action, to making things as right as possible.

Get some paper. Or flip open your laptop. Note what you're angry about, who you're angry with, and why. As you write down the circumstances behind why you get angry, you're beginning to channel that anger in the right direction.

Think about why you're angry related to your present struggle. Who are you angry with because of this setback? Why are you angry with them?

I recommend that you consider finding a mentor, or becoming part of a Restorative Small Group or Online Restorative Support Network. Then share what you've discovered about yourself with them.

"What if?" and "If only!"

We all do this. It's human. We think back on the failures in our lives and wonder what we—or others—could have done differently to have prevented them from happening. It can be useful to examine and reflect on the "What if's" and "If only's" you use when thinking about a particular failure.

If you intend to be accountable and to control what you can control, focusing on this impulse can help you plan to do things differently in the future, and so prevent failure. But *dwelling* on the "What if's" and "If only's" is not productive and does not promote accountability.

"What if's" and "If only's" create a victim mentality, where you believe that things simply happen to you. Because if you're not in control, why would you need to change and do things differently? You can spend a lot of time thinking about how others, or the situation, could have been different. But doing this doesn't change your circumstances today, and it doesn't change how you behave in the future.

Some people go way back whenever something negative happens in their lives, blaming their parent(s) or their upbringing. If you find yourself doing this, you might want to talk to a trained counselor to explore things on a deeper level.

As with many athletes, I have my "What if" and "If only" stories. I played football from the time I was five years old all the way through college. Most sports have those amazing moments that change a game. They make sports so exciting, but they also create the perfect environment for thinking about "What if" and "If only." Sports, particularly football, have been part of who I am for a long time. Even today, many years after football, I find myself thinking about certain moments in games that could have happened differently. All it takes is driving past a freshly cut field in August to take me back to one of those times.

One of my major "If only" occasions (that I still sometimes wake up in the middle of the night in a cold sweat thinking about) happened during my senior year of high school. Even as I share this story now, I find myself getting angry. It rouses my frustration and deep desire to go back to one particular moment. An instant when I lost the big game.

I was halfway through my senior year at Bethesda Chevy Chase (B-CC) High School in Bethesda, Maryland. Our team's record was three wins and one loss at the time. We were starting to get some recognition around the state for our success. We were playing in another high school's homecoming game. We were winning by a touchdown with one minute left in the game. All we had to do was run out the clock and the win was ours—we would advance to 4-1, which, for B-CC, was the best record in many years.

For anyone watching, it looked as though it should have been easy. The game was essentially over. I played center my senior year. The center's job is to snap the ball to the quarterback to start every play. With one minute left and winning by seven, we just had to snap the ball a couple more times and we would win, ruining the homecoming celebration for our opponent.

My buddies and I were talking trash to the other team, telling them how overrated they were. We were laughing as we walked up to the ball because the game was virtually over, and we had played hard and deserved the win. Why not enjoy the moment?

In the huddle the quarterback called a routine dive play for the fullback to get the ball and run up the middle. In football they call this running out the clock. It would probably be the last play of the game, and we could start celebrating.

The quarterback got down under me and started to yell, "Barons set hut!" When he said "hut," I snapped the ball and started to push the nose guard in front of me. I remember that everything sort of stood still. No one moved—except me and the player I was blocking. I started to hear loud cheers in the stands, and the man I was blocking started to cheer and jump up and down. I glanced backwards and saw someone running the other way with the ball.

Before I knew it, the other team ran the ball 80 yards the other way for a touchdown. I thought to myself, "What the hell just happened?!" The game was supposed to be over. We were about to run to the bus and start celebrating.

There was much discussion among the referees, and our coach was screaming his head off. Our quarterback finally came over to me and said the snap was to be on "Two." That was the moment when I realized this was all my fault.

I hadn't paid attention in the huddle. I assumed that our quarterback had said, "Twenty-two dive on one." But he had said, "Twenty-two dive on *two*." That may seem like a small detail—just a one-word difference—but it made all the difference in the world to what happened next.

When I snapped the ball on "one," our quarterback didn't move. He stood there holding the ball. But the other team did move, as they are allowed and trained to do. One of the defensive linemen moved across the line, and no one on our team moved to block him. They were still waiting for that second "hut." The opposing lineman took the ball out of our quarterback's hands and ran 80 yards the other way for a touchdown. The game went into overtime, and we lost by a touchdown in double overtime.

I've always wished that life was a little more like sports, because in sports, you know at all times where you stand in terms of success. With football, you walk away with a win or a loss once a week. This time we lost, and everyone knew it was because of me. To make matters worse, my whole family was in the stands, including my grandparents, the only game they were able to make all year.

Although everyone on our team knew what happened and knew the mistake I made, the fans didn't know. The whole play was confusing to them, and most of them were in disbelief that we had lost.

I remember walking to the team bus in shock, embarrassed, angry, and scared. When I got on the bus and took my seat I was thinking we should be celebrating, partying, singing. This bus ride should be the best bus ride ever! What happened? It took the longest time ever for me to change out of my uniform, get showered, and head home. I drove my buddy Ken to his house in silence. When I dropped him he said, "You know it's not your fault. The quarterback should have fallen on the ball. The play was live. He shouldn't have just stood there with the ball. Don't be so upset." I thanked him for his words but I knew better.

The dialogue already going on in my head, which would continue, was, "You loser, you idiot, you screwed it up for everyone. See, you're just a dumb little screw-up." I was holding myself accountable for a terrible lapse in concentration, in part because I was celebrating too early and not paying attention to doing my job.

The problem with self-talk that's not shared or checked is that it starts to turn into something much worse. After this game, I added to the ongoing self-talk I had been having with myself for a long time. It didn't end with "You screwed up. You lost the game." Instead, it grew into "You're a screw-up. You're a loser."

After I dropped my friend Ken off, I turned toward home. My family was waiting for me for dinner and what should have been a celebration. But I just

---

RESTORATIVE QUESTIONS

Name as many "What if" *and* "If only" moments from your life as you can.

———

What is the biggest regret you have in your life thus far?

couldn't imagine facing them, especially my Pap-Pap. He and my grandmother had driven all the way from Pittsburgh to Maryland to watch me play. I realized that not everyone at my house would understand what happened at the end and why we lost the game. So I was going to have to explain what I did and why we lost. I couldn't do it.

I pulled into a church parking lot and sat there. I was already in a very unhealthy place and was adding this failure to my running story. It went something like this: "You aren't good enough, strong enough, tough enough, smart enough. You can't do this. You're a little punk who can't be trusted."

In those days there were no cell phones, so I sat alone in the parking lot while my family back home wondered where in the hell I was. Finally I drove home slowly and faced the music. I told them what happened and tried to joke through the evening to hide the pain I was feeling.

One of my best friends Tony called me and said he heard that I thought I lost the game. He said, "No way. Rick [the quarterback] should have known the ball was live and fallen to the ground. It's not your fault. Come on, let's go to the party and forget about this." I appreciated what he was trying to do, but I knew better. A few more friends called to check on me and to try to talk me into going out that night. I finally relented and agreed to meet them. Everyone tried to cheer me up and tried to place the blame in other places—explaining how it shouldn't have been that close, that we still should have won in overtime, that the referees screwed us with a bad call in overtime. Sometimes other people come up with the "What if's" and "If only's" for you.

I used humor to act like I was okay and to get through the night. It wasn't until practice on Monday when things took a turn toward my recovering. The head coach, Pete White, a man I respected and admired tremendously, said in front of the whole team, "When you're the center on the offensive line, no one even knows your name. You do your job, and no one gives you credit for anything—unless you screw up big time. Then people know who you are. And of course, our quarterback hands the ball off to the other team."

The whole team laughed, and the great thing about football is we moved on. With football you have to—you can't dwell on the wins or the losses because in seven days there's another game to play.

My friends, the head coach, and our quarterback all helped me get through this moment in my young life. Our quarterback was a great leader and very quickly attempted to take the blame for what happened. I wish now I would have shared with a trusted mentor or a close friend what was going on in my head and what I felt like. I had not developed a strong support network and was not aware of my self-talk.

The problem with my inner dialogue at that critical stage of my life was that I didn't share my real thoughts and deep inner feelings with anybody. I (and the people I knew) used humor to get through tough times, but I never critically examined what was going on, what I was thinking about myself, or how I was making meaning of the mistakes and failures in my life. I was developing unhealthy ways of addressing failure and setbacks for the future. Those practices might help me get *through* tough times, but they would not help me *learn* from the tough times.

There is a huge difference. A Restorative Process can help you not only get through, but rise stronger, develop a healthy resilient identity, and, most importantly, develop a healthy framework for addressing failure for the rest of your life.

I was missing several things at that time: sharing my feelings with others, a support network, examining my self-talk, and self-care practices. I hadn't found someone to talk with authentically about what I was really thinking and feeling about myself. I never examined or reflected on how I understood the events in my life and what I said about myself. Instead of finding positive ways of taking care of myself during difficult times, I used unhealthy habits when responding to setbacks and failures—alcohol, distancing myself from others, hiding from hard situations, and not challenging myself.

My support people were well meaning and always trying to cheer me up, but I wasn't developing positive ways to be accountable for my failures. I either blamed others or my circumstances for my failures and made excuses for my behavior. I found it easier not to take the risk than to fail and hold myself accountable. I wasn't looking for mentors and role models who would help motivate me to be better, to become

> ### RESTORATIVE QUOTES
>
> *"Self-talk is the most powerful form of communication, because it either empowers you or defeats you."*
>
> UNKNOWN
>
> *"At some point you just have to let go of what you thought should happen and live in what is happening."*
>
> HEATHER HEPLER

the person I wanted to be, to find meaning and purpose in my life. I spent time with people who were doing the same things I was doing. We all lacked the experience and wisdom to help each other grow.

I spent many years developing negative, unhealthy habits, which led me to forming a negative identity. Breaking those habits and changing myself took time. Sharing, being authentic, and deeply examining my purpose—the "why I am here and what I was made to do for others"—would come much later.

Now when I wake up in the middle of the night after dreaming about the day I lost the big game nearly 30 years ago, I do think about "What if." If that had never happened, it's unlikely that I would understand other people's stories of failure. The story hasn't changed, but I've discovered new meaning in it. What if that had never happened? I probably would not be able to empathize with other people's anxiety and fears. Without that experience I would never have learned the importance of friendship, of helping people rise stronger from setbacks.

I am called upon to mentor college football players on a regular basis. My experiences have helped me relate and understand where they're coming from. I have learned and practice gratitude for all these past experiences, even the really tough ones. I think about "What if's," but I've changed my self-talk. I have shared my story—which I now understand differently. I am grateful for this moment in my life that allowed me to grow wiser.

When I was in high school, football was everything. Winning that game seemed so important. But now my perspective has become how grateful I am that the result of a game was my biggest worry and concern as I was growing up. I have worked with others who face hunger, life-threatening diseases, death of a parent, starvation, famine, even war. I was concerned about a football game—one game. I have learned the power of perspective and using self-talk to reframe the story in my head, putting what is going on in my life next to what is going on in the world.

There are many ways to gain perspective, and most come from getting out and living life, taking risks, and serving others. Reading history and biographies, especially about struggles that others have overcome, can change our viewpoints.

RESTORATIVE QUESTS

Create a mantra. Every time you start negative self-talk, replace it with a positive mantra. An example of a simple mantra can be "I am strong" or "I got this."

Keep a self-talk journal. Track your inner dialogue for a week. Write down all the things you find yourself saying to yourself. When do you say these things? What are the common themes in your self-talk? How can you catch your self-talk and turn it into something positive?

Only through living life, sharing our stories, and reflecting on our lives do we grow and become stronger.

Wisdom and learning are extremely different. Wisdom is gained by doing, applying what you've learned to life, experimenting, failing, and sharing with others. It comes as you find someone who has done what you want to do and learn from them, as you find someone who is being the person you want to be. When you discover this type of mentor and share with each other, you can change your story and begin to become wise.

CHAPTER THREE

The Ancient Art of Restorative Practices

"Sweet are the uses of adversity, which
like the toad, ugly and venomous, wears
yet a precious jewel in his head."

SHAKESPEARE

Howard Zehr, one of the pioneers of Restorative Justice, defines RJ as "A process to involve, to the extent possible, those who have a stake in a specific offense, and to collectively identify and address harms, needs, and obligations, in order to heal and put things as right as possible" (*The Little Book of Restorative Justice*).

Restorative Practices are a part of a process used to address conflict and healing with others in a community. The Restorative approach uses the principles of Restorative Justice to examine how our setbacks and failures create harm, needs, and obligations that we are responsible for, and how to make meaning of them in our lives. The Restorative approach also addresses the harm and needs we do to ourselves when we fail, and the obligations we have to make things as right as possible.

Restorative Practices are an ancient approach that builds community, addresses conflict, creates accountability, and engages people. I learned about Restorative Justice many years ago and used it in my work as Dean of Students. I was able to take a course on Restorative Justice taught by the legendary Howard Zehr. Howard embodies Restorative Justice in the way he lives and interacts with the world. Howard has been an amazing mentor to me over the years and truly helped mold me into the person I am today. When I first learned that building resiliency is premised on sharing, I immediately thought of Restorative Practices, which also encourage sharing stories. The pillars of Restorative Justice involve addressing the harms, needs, and obligations, caused by doing wrong to others (Zehr).

From working with thousands of students over the years, I have seen the harm caused by personal failures. I have met with students who are withdrawing from the university, who feel broken by setbacks they're experiencing. Their failure or series of failures have led them to believe that they are personally a failure, that they do not belong in college.

> According to 2018 and 2019 student surveys from the American College Health Association (ACHA), about 60% of respondents felt "overwhelming" anxiety, while 40% experienced depression so severe they had difficulty functioning.
>
> ACHA's 2018 survey indicated that 40% of American college students experienced at least one major depressive episode that year.

If any of us does not examine and make meaning of our setbacks, we are highly likely to develop a negative self-identity.

For the most part, our society's current culture of addressing failure is not moving in a healthy direction. We need to learn to share our struggle stories, discover what we can from our failures, and develop resiliency as a lifelong approach in response to life's setbacks. The need to restore ourselves from our setbacks and failures is critical to developing positive self-identity and learning how to grow. More people are depressed and experience anxiety than ever before. The need is urgent:

- ❖ 19% of adults experience mental illness.
- ❖ 4.34% of adults report serious thoughts of suicide.
- ❖ 13.84% of youth (ages 12-17) report suffering from at least one major depressive episode in the past year.

(from Mental Health America 2021)

This is not just a higher education problem. This is a cultural problem in our society. People tend to lack the bounce-back and grit to respond to life's setbacks and failures. If we are not encouraged to talk about our difficulties, and we don't share our stories, how can we grow and practice the skills necessary to develop resiliency? If social media encourages sharing just the best of ourselves, the positive parts of our lives, we won't find help there for making meaning of the setbacks and struggles in our lives. We need to equip ourselves with a process that helps us respond positively to the storms in our lives and assists us in using failure to develop a resilient mindset.

Restorative Justice allows space for storytelling, expressing emotions, cultivating accountability, engaging with others, and addressing harms, needs, and obligations to make things right. Using Restorative Practices to address the setbacks and failures in your life is a powerful way to become the person you say you want to be.

A true personal failure or setback usually creates harm to yourself and possibly to others. To heal, you need to recognize the various harms your actions have created, and then be accountable to make things as right as possible.

The harms also create needs—needs that have to be met, not only for yourself but for others. Things cannot go back to the way they were prior to your setback. But by reflecting on what you've done, and working to make things as right as possible, you—we—can become better, stronger people through the Restorative Process.

Many students I've met in my role as Dean of Students have come into my office at the lowest point in their young lives. I try to help them realize that all they can control is how they respond from this point forward. It is important to know that when we fail, we do have some control over the situation, not changing what happened, but how we respond from now on. There is hope in that, but we are still accountable to repair the harm we've created.

If we have someone to process the experience with us, and to walk with us through the steps of making things as right as possible, we can be restored. We cannot go back to the way things were before the failure, but we can come out of the process a different person. What makes that difference depends on how we examine and make meaning of the failure in our lives.

This is not just about addressing the current setback. It is also about learning a process for handling setbacks for the rest of our lives. It is a process with skills that must be practiced. There is no one right way to restore ourselves from setbacks and failures. As we each work through the Restorative Process, we will need to take risks, try new things, and decide what works best for us personally. The end goal is not only to respond to the latest setback or failure but to discover how we each best take care of setbacks and failures going forward.

RESTORATIVE QUOTE

"People will forget what you said, people will forget what you did, but people will never forget how you made them feel."

MAYA ANGELOU

Storytelling

Restorative Practices start with the nearly lost art of storytelling. In ancient times, our ancestors sat around a fire in a circle and told stories. During those long hours of trying to stay warm, they shared wisdom and information, generation after generation. The stories we tell about our failures and setbacks become a part of who we are. Our stories show how we have made meaning from our setbacks and how they all are a part of our larger life stories.

Part of my job in higher education has been to meet with students who have violated university policy. Most of the time these are minor alcohol infractions or disorderly conduct. But there are a surprising number of major behavioral issues with drugs, violence to persons, sexual assaults, and other dangerous practices. Sometimes students violate the law in the surrounding community and are detained in jail. If students are arrested for underage drinking, the standard practice is to hold them overnight in jail until they sober up and release them the next day. Some take until the afternoon of the next day to sober up. If it was a serious violation, I would go to the local jail and meet with the student to tell them they had been temporarily suspended from the university, pending a full hearing for their offense.

Another typical serious wrongdoing is assaulting a police officer, along with public drunkenness. When students are extremely drunk, they often don't remember what they did the night before. I explain what landed them in jail and what they're facing going forward. This quickly gets most students' attention.

I remember one student in particular. I received a phone call at 3:00 a.m., informing me that John had assaulted a city police officer and was being held in jail without bond. I drove the 10-minute trip to the downtown local jail.

Over the years I found it important to call one of the officers on the scene who had witnessed the assault to get a firsthand account. In this case the officer explained that John was walking down the street by himself, tripped on the curb, and fell into the street. The officer was driving by and stopped to check on him. John was extremely intoxicated and under 21, the legal age requirement to consume alcohol.

In the course of the officer attempting to help him, John, in his intoxicated state, thought it best to attempt to push the officer and run to freedom. You can imagine how this went. He didn't get very far, and when the officer caught up with him and stopped his escape attempt, John elbowed the officer in his nose. The force was strong enough to cut the officer's nose, and he bled profusely. Now John was facing a felony assault on an officer, underage drinking, drunkenness in public, and disorderly conduct charges. Not the type of behavior a freshman in college wants to experience during his first month in school.

Having obtained the details, I showed up at the jail and witnessed his admittance into the county jail. The jailers and I knew each other quite well. Often after a big weekend, I recognized many of our students in the jail cells as I walked by. On homecoming weekend, I often saw alumni who waved and shouted, "Hi Dr. Bacon, how have you been? Can you get me out of here?"

This time the jailer said, "Sorry to get you out of bed, but this one is a pitiful case. He's in cell number two." The student was no longer "John," the freshman student majoring in biology. He was now referred to as "prisoner number 109 in the orange jumpsuit."

When I got these types of calls in the middle of the night and was racing to the jail, all kinds of thoughts went through my head, particularly early in my career. I imagined that this guy must be a monster, running from the police, pushing an officer, elbowing him in the face.

Over the years I learned that, if the student had had a chance to sleep off the alcohol by the time I showed up, I was usually greeted with a pathetic sight. These students don't look or act like monsters. After a night locked up in a cell, they're pretty broken and sad-looking. Most of the time they don't remember anything that happened the night before, or, at best, the details are extremely fuzzy for them. I found it best to be direct—to tell them what happened and what they were facing. Imagine a 3.0 GPA Biology major learning for the first time that s/he is facing felony assault charges on an officer and is being immediately suspended from their first choice of colleges. You get the picture. There are usually tears and a great deal of disbelief. At some point the student quickly realizes, "What am I going to tell my parents?" Or in John's case, "I have to be in biology class in four hours."

Once I informed John that he was not going to be making his 11:00 a.m. biology class, here is where my attempt to be straightforward and hold a student accountable would take a small turn. John immediately expressed disbelief, "What if's," and "This can't be." He first said, "I don't even really drink alcohol."

I let John walk me through his fuzzy version of the night's events. While sobbing, he said, "I was studying for my biology quiz when my suitemates came into my room with a bottle of vodka. They convinced me to take a break from my studies and have just one shot. I lost count after my twelfth shot. I remember going to a party with my suitemates, but after that I don't remember a thing. I've never been in a fight in my life. . . . My uncle's a police officer. . . . What am I going to do?" John seemed to sober up very rapidly at this point. The hopelessness of his situation was quickly setting in for him, as well as a belief that his life as he knew it was taking a major turn.

I've found it useful for students to experience this moment and let it soak in a little bit. Restorative Justice practitioners would call this moment "leaning into the fire." As humans, we tend to want to help people feel better right away and not suffer. It's a very natural human response to try to cheer someone up. But sometimes learning takes experiencing a little pain and suffering, particularly for people who have not experienced much pain and suffering up to this point in their lives. After letting him sit with the reality that he had made a mistake, I knew it was important to give him some hope and let him understand that he had some control. I told John, "You can control what you do from this point forward. You can't take away what happened last night, and you can't take away the bad choices you made throughout the evening. You can only decide what you do now."

Developing a plan for moving forward starts with accountability. The night in jail, when students still have alcohol in their systems, might not be the best time to start this process. But I like to remind students with this: "As soon as any of us can start taking accountability for our setbacks, the sooner we can start moving forward and making meaning of our failure."

It's unproductive to go back and think about "What if's" from our setback and failure. It's equally unhelpful to list all the ways others were to blame for our mistakes and failures. So let's start by controlling what we are accountable for. Think about how we can make things as right as possible from this point forward.

Our process and plan start with listing all the harms that were caused by our setback, mistake, failure, and bad decisions. We need to acknowledge not only the harms that have already affected us and our lives, but also the harms that others experienced because of our decisions and behaviors.

In John's case, his harms may include:

- ❖ His own reputation
- ❖ His relationship with his parents (trust)
- ❖ His relationship with his university
- ❖ The officer he assaulted
- ❖ The professors whose classes he'll be missing

As any of us gains experience by going through this process of listing harms, along the way we come to realize that we can go even deeper.

John had more harms to consider:

- ❖ The role alcohol is going to play in his life from this point forward
- ❖ His roommate who is now alone

❖ The student staff who live in the residence hall and helped him through the beginning of the semester

❖ His ability to get a government job, join the military, or secure other future employment (potentially having to put "felony" on all applications)

❖ His education

❖ Other parts of his future

As we can see when we experience a setback and failure, it creates harm to oneself. And when we dig deeper, we see how our actions do not just affect ourselves, but also others.

John had a long, hard road ahead as he recovered from what he had done. He caused a lot of harm to himself and others, and he needed to be held accountable for making things right. John was suspended from the university, but his charge was eventually lowered, and he never did any jail time, other than that Thursday night when he should have been in his dorm room studying for a biology quiz.

I saw John many years later, and he approached me. I am never sure in these cases if a former student is going to walk up and punch me in the face or hug me. In his case, he wanted to thank me. He said, "As hard as this experience was, it was what I needed to appreciate how important an education was in my life." He told me that he transferred schools and completed his biology degree elsewhere.

John reflected that he can't forget his night in jail and his meeting with me, but he said he remembers it as a place he never wants to be again, that it motivated him every time he was studying in the future. He recalled,

RESTORATIVE QUESTION

Can you think of any negative setback or failure in your life that maybe needed to happen to teach you a lesson or to make you better?

"Years later my friends knew what I valued and how important my education was. So they did not dare come into my room on a weekday while I was studying and ask me to take a shot."

◆ ◆ ◆

HARM

Naming the harm you have experienced and created for others because of your failure is an important step in being accountable for your actions. List all the ways your failure has caused harm in your life. Naming harms gives you control so you can find a starting place for making things better. Then you can address the harms you have experienced and the harms you have caused to yourself and others. This is how you heal, and not only heal, but grow, learn, and thrive.

My involvement with Restorative Practices led me to work in my local community and to help facilitate Restorative responses to potential criminal behaviors in my town. I worked with a group of people who helped bring these practices to the schools, the police department, the colleges in the area, and the criminal system. Our goal was to create a Restorative City. You can find people interested in Restorative Justice usually at higher education institutions, people working in the criminal justice system, and juvenile justice systems.

Our very first case, referred by the police department, involved an incident with two brothers who owned a small business in the town mall. The older brother—I'll call him Ronny—reported to the police that someone had stolen several phones from their store. The police investigated the incident by pulling video footage from the mall cameras. They found that an employee had taken the phones from the store, walked to a cell phone return booth down the mall, and sold them there. The video footage identified the employee as Ronny's younger brother Tyronne.

When the police informed the owner what had happened, he was shocked—and was confronted with the difficult option of charging Tyronne with theft. Since these cell phones were valued at thousands of dollars, it would be a felony charge with five to 10 years potential jail time.

The arresting officer had just gone through the Restorative Justice training the City RJ group delivered. After talking with Ronny, who did not want to place felony charges, the officer let him know about another option—Restorative Justice. The case was referred to me by the case management team of the City RJ program, and we started the process.

I met first with Ronny, the victim and store owner. He reviewed with me what had happened, but he also told me his own story. Ronny had been arrested many years earlier and spent time in jail. He had been a star athlete in high school with multiple scholarship offers for football and track. But when Ronny was arrested for selling drugs, he lost all his scholarship offers and spent three years in jail.

Ronny did not want Tyronne to have to face the path he had to make for himself after jail. Ronny also told me about how their mother had passed away when they were young kids, and that they had never dealt with her death. He believed Tyronne was still struggling with this.

I am amazed that if you create the right space for sharing, people will tell you the deeper parts of their stories. When I met with Ronny, he asked, what if his mom hadn't passed away? What if he hadn't sold drugs? What if he hadn't been arrested, and had instead taken one of the scholarship offers? What if he hadn't spent three years in prison?

In this case, asking "What if's" helped Ronny make a decision about what he wanted Tyronne to learn from the recent experience. He had just turned 18 and was about to graduate high school.

Ronny still wanted to hold his brother accountable. He didn't want him thinking that this was no big deal and that he could just go on about his life. He wanted him to gain wisdom, wisdom that Ronny wished he had had many years ago, prior to some of the decisions he made.

Ronny was wise—he had clearly done the hard work of reflecting on his life while in prison, and the decisions he had made. When Ronny left prison, he struggled for many years to get—and keep—a job. He had discovered that owning his own business allowed him the freedom to make a difference in other people's lives, particularly his brother's.

I met with Tyronne and talked about the Restorative Process and what it would look like. I explained that he, along with Ronny and I, would sit in a circle to talk about what happened, the harms that were created, the needs that now needed to be made right, the younger brother's obligations to the needs, and how he could engage in a process to heal his relationship with his older brother. Because the other option was likely criminal charges, he was willing to do this.

I listened to Tyronne's story of what had happened. Although he was very nervous and concerned about sitting down with Ronny and telling him what he did, he was willing to try. Several days later the three of us met together in my office.

Tyronne told his story of what happened. He explained that he wasn't being paid enough by his older brother. Now that he was 18, he needed more money to pay his expenses.

Ronny told his story of what had happened to him years earlier, and the effects of going to prison. He explained that he did not want Tyronne to face the burden of a felony theft charge the rest of his life. At the same time, he wanted him to learn that if he continued to steal, Ronny would press charges, and prison would be the only place he'd be going.

When conducting Restorative Processes over the years, I am still surprised when at some point, things go from being surface to deeper, to getting at the roots of the problems, to where people start being open and honest and speaking from their hearts. These were two very tough men who had led difficult lives. They were brothers, but it seemed they had never really talked deeply about life.

Tyronne appreciated Ronny and respected him tremendously. We reached the point during our meeting when things shifted from a surface level discussion to something much deeper. People are usually craving more meaningful relationships, so if you create the right Restorative environment, they often become willing to share deeply with others.

Ronny opened up about the death of their mother and apologized to his brother for never talking about it with him. He asked him if he needed counseling and if he wanted help.

Through tears, Tyronne talked about the day their mother passed away and how lost he had been ever since. He shared the challenges he was now facing. Their father had cut him off because he turned 18. He feared facing a future without their mom. He had no prospect for college and no financial means to support himself.

This was the first time these two brothers had ever talked together about their mother's death. They shared tears, they shared their fears, and they grew closer. They talked about how they could move forward together and support each other.

Ronny didn't let his brother off the hook. Together they planned all the ways Tyronne would address the harm he had caused. He would make monthly payments to pay for the cell phones he stole. He would also meet with me once a week for two months so I could mentor him, help him examine his life, and talk about the possibility of college in his future.

I'm not sure what would have happened if Ronny had chosen to charge his brother with a felony theft and they had gone through the criminal process. I do know that after the brothers met, Tyronne applied to the local community college. I also kept in touch with Ronny and was glad to see he was growing his business. He had a desire to help others who were in similar situations as himself. He offered to become involved in the city Restorative Justice program and become a mentor to others.

Ronny gained a tremendous amount of wisdom from this experience, and he was willing to share and serve others. Because he had spent time reflecting on his own failures, he wanted to make things right in his community by helping others.

Ronny was able to articulate the harms that Tyronne had caused him. Together they were able to identify the harms that Tyronne had created for himself. By going through a Restorative Process, the brothers found space to share their emotions with each other and to look at the roots of some of their issues. Both brothers came to realize the harms and needs that developed in their family when their mother passed away. From the Restorative Process, they realized they had obligations to each other. Together they created a plan for addressing them. This process was extremely healing for both brothers, and they grew even closer.

Tyronne began counseling so he could deal with his emotional difficulties, which had gone unchecked due to the death of his mother.

Restorative possibilities

When you create a space to be restorative, and hold yourself accountable for action, you can begin to honestly address the harms that you caused or have experienced. Listing your harms is an important first step. There is no one right way to do this. Here are two restorative possibilities:

1. **Restorative Mentor:** After a relationship has been formed and some trust has been established between a mentor and a person who's

caused or experienced harm, the two sit together and review the story of the setback.

The person being mentored can brainstorm all the harms that have been created. The mentor can encourage and challenge them to dig deeper to name all the possible harms.

In the first stages, brainstorm as many as possible. Don't edit yourself. Just get them all down. You can review and change later.

RESTORATIVE QUESTS

List all the harms that your most recent setback has **created for yourself.**

List all the harms that your most recent setback has **created for others.**

---

2.   **Restorative Small Group:** In this powerful experience, everyone participating can learn, grow, and help others learn how to hold themselves accountable for the harm they caused. Once a Restorative environment is created, the group can challenge each other to dig deeper, be accountable, and name all the harms that have been caused. Everyone can learn how to look at their own situation and story and hold themselves accountable.

Belonging to a group of people who care about each other and are willing to hold each other accountable can restore and lead to a tremendous amount of growth. The process should happen in a caring manner, rather than being accusatory. I call it "giving truth with love." Use the Restorative Practice of creating a designated space for difficult discussions. For example, ask everyone to sit in a circle with nothing between you. You can place a centerpiece on the floor that is symbolic for the group.

To make this a Circle Process, identify a "talking piece" that is meaningful to the group. Only the person holding the talking piece may speak. Whoever has the talking piece has everyone's undivided attention and respect. When someone finishes speaking, that person passes the talking piece to their neighbor, and so on, giving every-one an equal chance to contribute. Everyone has the right to pass the talking piece on without speaking. (More about Circle Processes on pages 76-77.)

NEEDS

"What if every bad thing that's ever happened to you—including every problem you ever had— was there, in your life, to get you in touch with abilities you never knew you had?"

UNKNOWN

Moving from naming harms to addressing the needs they've created is the next important step. Holding yourself accountable for the harms you caused to yourself and others is an important way to empower yourself to be accountable, manage what you can control, and begin to better yourself from the experience.

To make things as right as possible, you will identify obligations for yourself. That means digging deep enough to see the needs that result from the harms. Look at the history of how failure fits into your life story. Recognizing the needs for yourself is how you begin to use the setback as a means to grow stronger and wiser.

> **Needs** are caused by harms. Other deeper needs are exposed by harms.
>
> **Obligations** are the actions that need to be taken to make things as right as possible.

Many years ago, I was teaching a college course when a student asked to speak to me after class. Because I was Dean of Students, that was very common. Students would ask anything from directions to the bathroom to launching a deep discussion about a major life issue.

We sat down on a bench, and he began to tell me his story. This student was a fifth-year senior, about to graduate in two weeks, and he wanted to talk about something that happened five years before during his freshman year. I'll call him James. James said that in his first year of college he came out as gay. This was a huge step in James's life. The first weekend after he came out to his friends, an incident occurred that had affected him for the past four years.

He was at a party on a Thursday night at his very close friend's house. James said he was not drinking and did not plan to stay long because he had a test the next morning. Then two of his close friends called him upstairs to discuss something important with him. They told him that they were very concerned about Eric, another student in their group of friends.

They believed Eric was gay, and now that James had come out, they wanted to see if James would talk to Eric about his sexuality. In fact, the friends were wanting to have some fun and embarrass Eric by creating this situation.

James told his two friends that it was up to Eric when and with whom to discuss his sexuality. But if Eric came to him, he'd be open to talking about it with him. The two friends went to Eric and confronted him about his sexuality. They said that James wanted to talk to him about it.

James noticed later in the evening that Eric was drinking very heavily and seemed to be getting out of control. A couple of hours later James decided to leave and get some sleep before his exam, so he started to say his goodbyes. The party had moved outside, and James was walking off the porch, headed to his car. Eric jumped toward him, and in front of everybody yelled, "Hey, faggot," to James. When James turned around, Eric punched him in the face. James's glasses flew off, and he felt a sharp pain in his jaw. He grabbed his glasses and ran to his car.

James said that after that he never talked to Eric again and avoided his other friends who were present that night. James said that every time he saw Eric after the incident, he was terrified and attempted to avoid him over the next four years. James explained that he had been living with this terrible experience since then, and at the time it happened, he assumed that this was what the rest of his life would be like.

When James finished, I put on my Director of Student Conduct hat and started to talk about all the options available to him. I said that we could go to the police about criminal charges. We could press "violence to persons" charges through the university.

James shook his head. He wasn't interested in any of that but wanted to hear more about the Restorative Justice Process I discussed in class. At the time I was just learning about Restorative Justice, and I was excited to talk about it. I had mentioned the Process and how it was used to address conflict and harm. James said he wanted to try Restorative Justice. He was about to graduate, and so was Eric. James had been living with this fear for the past four years, and he just wanted to know why the incident had happened.

Since Restorative Justice was new to me at the time, I was still somewhat skeptical of its effectiveness. I was far more comfortable with our traditional criminal and conduct processes. I made sure to report the incident to Title IX and offer James all the services that were appropriate. But if he as the survivor did not want to utilize any of the traditional processes and was choosing Restorative Justice, I decided to honor his wishes.

I met with James again and explained all his options and what the Restorative Process would entail. Together we brainstormed the possible obligations for Eric that we could include during our meeting. After that I called Eric. As soon as I introduced myself and started to talk about why I was calling, Eric interrupted me and said, "I know exactly why you're calling. This has been bothering me for the past four years, and I would love to meet with James."

I met with Eric in my office and explained the Restorative Process. I was quick to inform him that there still could be criminal and university conduct charges in the future. Eric was a good candidate to participate in the Restorative Process because he was admitting responsibility, was being accountable for his actions, wanted to apologize, and was open to making things as right as possible from this point forward. We were nearing the end of the school year; both students were scheduled to graduate in two weeks.

A Restorative Circle Process

We decided that I would facilitate a Restorative Circle Process with James, Eric, a support person for each, and myself. To guide the discussion, we used a "talking piece"—in this case, the University Centennial Medallion. The rules for the talking piece are that whoever is holding it is the only one who may speak. Whoever is speaking is to have everyone's attention and respect when they are speaking. When it's your turn, you can either speak, or pass the talking piece on to your neighbor without speaking if you prefer. The talking piece will come back to you if you decide you want to talk later.

For the Circle Process, we planned several rounds of questions. In the first round, the opening question was designed to develop relationships among the participants. In the following rounds, the questions were framed around the pillars of Restorative Justice.

❖ **Round One:** Tell us your story related to this incident.

❖ **Round Two:** What **harms** were created?

❖ **Round Three:** What **needs** are now present for everyone involved?

❖ **Round Four:** What **obligations** do you have to make things right?

❖ **Round Five:** We developed a contract related to the obligations, and asked everyone involved if they could agree to meet these expectations.

When the talking piece was passed to Eric for him to tell his story, he said this was not the first time his sexuality was questioned. He had always been angry and embarrassed by this. So the fact that two of his close college friends were now asking him really upset him.

He said he drank way too much that night. He figured that the most masculine thing he could do to show everybody that he was not gay was to beat James up and call him a faggot. He said his drunken state was not an excuse, but it gave him the courage to act on his misguided plan.

Eric said that since the incident, he had always wanted to apologize to James, but he was so upset and embarrassed about what he had done that he was afraid to. When he heard James say that since then, he lived with the fear that this is what his life was going to be like after coming out, Eric broke down in tears. While crying, Eric shared that during the first weekend of his first year on campus, he went out to a party and was sucker-punched. It turned out that the guy who did it thought Eric was somebody else. Eric lived in fear ever since that that guy would hurt him again. Eric said that after hearing James tell his story, he realized he had done the same thing to James.

This was empathy in action. In tears, Eric apologized to James. "This was about me wanting to show people I was a man, and I didn't think at all about you. I'm so sorry I did this to you."

When the talking piece got back again to James, he thanked Eric for his apology and said the whole experience had helped him understand what he was afraid of—that this is what his life would be like forever. "Now I know this had nothing to do with me. It was all about you and not me."

James had a list of potential obligations he wanted Eric to do, but he said, "I think I finally have the closure I needed. I wish we could have talked a long time ago."

I had conducted discipline meetings and addressed student behavior for 20 years, but I had never seen students talk to each other like this in conduct processes. I had never seen male students have a discussion like this about sexuality. And they did it all in front of me. I had rarely ever seen students apologize to each other or walk away satisfied from a conduct process.

A few days later I received two thank-you notes in the campus mail. Both students sent me letters, thanking me for facilitating the process and for helping them get closure from the incident so many years ago. I can count on one hand how many thank-you letters I have received from conducting the university judicial process.

Restorative Practices create a space for open, honest sharing to: a) meet the victim's needs, b) hold the responding person accountable, c) involve the community in the process as much as possible, d) get at the deeper roots of why the harm was caused, and e) make things as right as possible.

When we first began this at the university, I was involved in conducting all the Restorative Processes because I couldn't believe they would all go this well. I wanted to see what happened when they didn't go well. I'm pleased to report that none **ever** went badly. They were not all as emotional and powerful as James's and Eric's Circle Process, but I found that people, in general, are craving this type of connection.

RESTORATIVE QUESTIONS

List all the needs that your most recent setback has created.

_____

What are the needs of others who have been affected by your most recent failure?

Initially when I explained Restorative Justice to people, they were skeptical and said, "No way students are going to sit in a circle and share like that. They text their roommate when they have a problem." I admit I was skeptical at first, too. But I found that people want this type of connection and accountability, and college students will rise to the occasion if given the opportunity. Creating a different space, away from technology and other distractions, connects us in a way that our ancestors used—sitting in a circle focused on each other.

> ## RESTORATIVE QUOTE
>
> *"I want to try making things right because picking up the pieces is way better than leaving them the way they are."*
>
> SIMONE ELKELES, PERFECT CHEMISTRY

The harms we cause ourselves and others when we experience setbacks create needs. One need is to address the harm we created. Another is to make things right to the extent possible. This begins the healing process and gives us hope that we can rise from this setback stronger.

Often when we explore the needs that have been created, we begin to see the needs in our life that were not being met prior to the setback. We can start to actually address the root needs in our lives that may have led to the failure. By examining and then working towards meeting our own needs, and the needs of others, we begin to experience accountability for owning our setback and taking control of our lives from this point forward.

◆ ◆ ◆

OBLIGATIONS

- ❖ What obligations do I have to the people whom I have harmed to make things as right as possible?
- ❖ How can I make things as right as possible?
- ❖ What obligations do I have to myself moving forward?

Addressing my obligations moves me toward being accountable and taking action, which ultimately leads me to being a person with integrity. These steps help me to become the kind of person I say I want to be. As I work toward meeting my obligations related to a specific event, I begin to change the self-talk in my head. Meeting my obligations requires action. It also can lead me to having a positive self-image which might have been damaged during a setback.

Let's revisit John's incident and determine all the harms and the needs that resulted from his assault on the police officer.

The police officer needs to heal from the incident, not only physically, but also emotionally, from the trauma he experienced. The officer may have a negative view of college students. John needs to determine what role he can play to meet the needs of the officer and his family's concern for his safety. This can be a tricky process. Others who become involved may be working toward other goals and ends. For example, John's attorney, and even his parents, will likely try to do damage control. They're inclined to have John face as few consequences as possible, including mitigating future damage. Attorneys tend not to have their client admit responsibility nor apologize to the people who have been harmed due to their actions.

When I talk with parents, I first ask what their ultimate goal is. How do they want this experience to fit into their son's or daughter's life story?

I believe that damage control and limiting consequences as much as possible may *not* be the best approach to helping a person learn, grow, change, and become the person they ultimately want their child to be.

Our current systems and immediate responses tend to lead away from persons fulfilling their obligations and making things as right as possible. Our systems often give people the false sense that they are not fully accountable or responsible for their actions, and that someone is ready to catch them every time they fail.

I often hear—and observe—that many college students—or many people in general—feel entitled. I have found that reviewing one's obligations promotes the opposite of entitlement. Instead of asking, "What do I get, and what do I deserve," addressing one's obligations is about, "What do I owe myself, others, my community, and the world?"

Helping change someone's mindset from one of entitlement to one of accountability is possible if we remember that we are helping a person address their current setback or failure. In addition, we are giving them a process for addressing all setbacks and failures restoratively in the future.

Is your ultimate goal to have them face as few negative consequences as possible, or to help them become the person they say they want to be? Imagine a world where people are routinely thinking about all their obligations in life.

- ❖ What are my obligations to my partner?
- ❖ What are my obligations to my family, my parents, and my children?
- ❖ What are my obligations to my colleagues and to my employer?
- ❖ What are my obligations to the community I live in?
- ❖ What are my obligations to my country, the environment, and to the world?

My discussions with college students nearing graduation and seeking employment often begin with the students focusing initially on what they expect *from* an employer. How much vacation time and how much money? Where is the most desirable place they can live? What can they get out of the job? Their focus for that first job after college is on the job's perks.

What about all the things they plan to *give* to the company? What about their *obligations*? What kind of *employee* do they plan to be during their lifetime?

My grandfather, whom we called Pap-Pap, was a role model for fulfilling obligations and giving back to others. Pap-Pap worked for the same company, United States Steel in Pittsburgh, Pennsylvania, for 40 years. His life seemed to revolve around "the Mill." I remember that after he retired, everywhere we went people stopped him, and they discussed what was happening at the Mill.

When my Pap-Pap wasn't working at the mill, he was a volunteer firefighter. It didn't matter what time of day or night it was, if the alarm went off, Pap-Pap went to help. It was what the community needed, and people like my Pap-Pap were there to respond. He was also committed to the church, and, every Sunday, no matter what, he and his family were there.

One of the most impressive things about him was that in 40 years of working in a steel mill, he never missed a day of work. This absolutely amazes me. I think of so many people now who cannot go even a month without a day off from work. Pap-Pap was my hero and one of my role models for what hard work and meeting one's obligations are all about.

What are my obligations?

Obligations start with this basic question regarding the setback just experienced: "How do I make things as right as possible from this point forward?" This question sets the tone for accountability, ownership, and control. It starts with self-action instead of blaming other people or demanding what others should do, including helping you get out of your situation.

It is essential to own the fact that you created this situation, and that it is up to you to make things right. It is important that you look at the list of harms and needs you caused, and then create another list of obligations that meet these needs and address the harms.

To be accountable, it is useful to include very specific actions and steps you will undertake to make things right. It is one thing to say "I'm sorry," to admit responsibility, or to describe what you are going to change. But it is far more important to take action and begin making things right. By taking action you acknowledge that you have failed. And you show your community through your behavior that you are accountable and changing for the better.

Admitting your obligations shows that you mean to take full responsibility for what you've done. Determining your obligations should be an ongoing endeavor, both when you have stumbled or caused harm, but also proactively, as a way of living your life. When you look at your obligations proactively, you develop a lifelong practice of offering service to others, to your profession and your community, and to our world. When you take responsibility for your obligations, you begin to experience that setbacks and failures can actually lead to growth and making things better.

Over the years I've worked with many athletes at the collegiate level. I am often asked to mentor a student athlete who has failed or caused major harm. What makes these cases somewhat unique is that the public is often very aware of the athlete's transgression. An athlete who's gotten in trouble or made a mistake is often in the headlines the next day. So now you have an 18- to 21-year-old student athlete who has the responsibility of picking themselves back up and moving forward, but doing so under the microscope of the entire university community and often far beyond. I've learned this commonly adds more shame for the student to bear.

Many years ago I worked with a star football player who made some mistakes off the field. The athlete's public persona was that he was extremely strong, competent, and tough. These outward characteristics always remind me of what I tried to be in college. He was sent to me so I would "help him through this experience." The athlete very quickly opened up to me about his current situation, his past life, and the shame he was feeling due to the incident. I was interested in how quickly he broke down and shared very personal information about his life.

I asked, "Who do you normally share these types of things with?" He answered, "Only you," and began to sob.

I have seen the power of sharing. The people who society deems the strongest and most confident are often the ones who most need an outlet in which to share the truth about themselves. I tried not to let my face register how sad I felt that he only had *me*, a person he had met just three times before, whom he was comfortable sharing with. This athlete was carrying many burdens, including the shame of his recent transgression, all by himself, while trying to maintain the cool, calm, leader persona that was expected of him as a star football player. It was more than he could handle.

A Restorative approach uses ancient practices to create a space that allows for healing, accountability, and making things as right as possible. You can rise stronger from setbacks and failures by following these. You can also practice this time-tested way of responding to setbacks for the rest of your life—and help someone else respond restoratively to a current failure of their own.

> ## RESTORATIVE QUESTIONS
>
> *List all the obligations* you have to make things right, or as right as possible.
>
> ———————
>
> *Is there a service* project you can do to make things right, that is connected to the harm you caused?

◆ ◆ ◆

ENGAGEMENT

"It is not only for what we do that we are held responsible, but also for what we do not do."

JEAN-BAPTISTE POQUELIN, KNOWN ALSO AS MOLIÈRE

One of the pillars of Restorative Justice is engagement. When using Restorative Justice to address conflict and harms, engagement includes, to the extent possible, making things right for all those people affected by the conflict. The Restorative Process uses sharing as a means of engagement in order to rise stronger from our setbacks.

Sharing is critical to recovering from setbacks and failures, and also critical in changing us from a culture where "no one fails," to embracing failure as part of the learning and developmental processes we all need to experience.

Sharing can take many forms, but a good starting place is by telling your story to a trusted mentor, the person you've chosen to walk with you through *The Restorative Practices Journal*, or by telling your struggle story to your Small Group. In my experience, when students are ready, as they're working through *The Restorative Practices Journal*, they often take the opportunity to share their own recovery story online

RESTORATIVE PRACTICES

A Restorative thank you: Think of someone from your past and thank them for helping you. Write a letter, send an email, or set up a meeting. Who from your past helped to make you better?

A Restorative apology: Identify someone from your past who you need to apologize to. Write a note, send an email, or meet with them in person to apologize.

with their Restorative Community. This is part of the Restorative and giving-back process, and it is also a part of changing our culture.

Sharing with a trusted individual, particularly someone who has already gone through the Restorative Process, helps build trust and takes away the shame we often experience with failure. Knowing that you are sharing to help others, while at the same time joining a community, helps us rise stronger and feel we are connected to a bigger purpose.

Fulfilling obligations means applying what you have learned thus far by going to those involved and making things as right as possible. This is important, first, when addressing your current setback, and then as an important life-long skill. Look at the world and determine your obligations in it. Make a list of the many roles you have in life. Then list all the obligations you have for those roles. Here is a list of roles and people to whom you might have obligations:

- ❖ Partner/spouse
- ❖ Family: My immediate family of origin
- ❖ Family: The people I consider my family now
- ❖ Spiritual community or church
- ❖ Employer
- ❖ Co-workers

Obligations to these people may increase if you have to make a particular setback right. Brainstorm, along with your Restorative Mentor or in your Restorative Small Group, all the ways you can address the harms and needs you may have created to these people if you've had a setback that affects them. You can also go directly to the people most closely related to the incident to come up with the obligations together.

The point is for you to offer and to attempt to make things as right as possible. We say "as right as possible" because some harm can never be completely taken back. Some things can never return to the way they were before. All of us have to live with this, that as much as we want to fix things and want people to forget what has happened, we cannot and they cannot. It is a part of their story and our story now.

I have found that "talk is cheap" when someone tries to make things as right as possible, and to be accountable for their obligations, simply by talking. The more severe the harm, the more people don't care what you say. They want to see action.

In fact, talking about what a good person you are, and talking about how you are never going to do it again, tends to cause more harm. This is the hard part, this is the grind, this is when you control what you can from this point forward. This is when you show people and the world that your failure does not define you. From now on, you have the opportunity to be accountable and to take responsibility for your life. Your new motto can be, "Talk is cheap. Just watch me." Or "I am going to show how I take care of my obligations."

Over the years, I have worked with students, particularly athletes, who had very public transgressions. In today's culture, this is amplified by their presence on social media. When their failure becomes public, everyone seems to give their opinion of what kind of person they are and what punishment they deserve.

If you're the offender, your impulse is likely to defend yourself, to tell everyone about all the good things you've done, and to share your side of the story. I have not seen positive results happen when offenders tell their side of the story and defend themselves on social media.

The important part of restoring the harm you have caused is to engage to the extent possible directly with the people most involved. At some point you may be able to give a public apology, or to publicly acknowledge the harm you caused. But done in the heat of the moment, it often looks like excuses and minimization.

"Watch me from this point forward."

An athlete whom I was mentoring was very set on defending himself and his family. His attorneys really wanted to make public statements to counter the negative comments in the press and on social media. Once I developed a relationship with this student athlete, I shared from past experience that the best thing to do when asked about what happened (and he was going to be asked a lot) is just to say, "Watch me from this point forward."

This became almost like a mantra for him during difficult times. It reminded him that he could only control his actions going forward. He didn't make excuses for the past. Instead, his short statement was forward looking. This was the beginning of this athlete's positive self-talk. He was changing his inner voice.

Of course, when you say, "Watch me from this point forward," you need to actually do something different from then on. It is one thing to say it, and that's the start of accountability. But then you have to let the world see through your actions that you are doing the right thing. Even if you are not in the public eye and the media isn't following your every step, some people are watching, particularly the people you harmed and the people to whom you have obligations. A constant goal in life can be showing the kind of person you want to be through your actions, not just your words.

Your actions should be guided by your mission statement, values, and vision. *The Restorative Practices Journal* will help guide you through creating a Mission Statement (see pages 106-107, 141, 211), listing your values (see pages 142, 212), and writing your vision (see pages 142, 212-213). When you start saying, "Just watch me," you are letting others know that you are accountable for what you do from this point forward. It should also be a reminder to yourself that "Talk is cheap" and that you are doing hard work.

One of my favorite athletes to watch has been Marshawn Lynch who played football for Seattle. You might remember that when his team went to the Super Bowl, he refused to talk to the media. Only when he was told that he'd be fined thousands of dollars did he appear before the Super Bowl's media spotlight. And then he simply said, "I'm here so I don't get fined."

Only when Deion Sanders (another athlete who focused on action and backed it up to the highest degree) approached Marshawn casually, with the cameras running, did Marshawn engage. He repeated to Deion Sanders, "I'm just bout dat action, Boss."

This quickly became a slogan and was printed on t-shirts around the country. I have one myself and I love it! It says, "That's right, talk is cheap. I'm just bout dat action, Boss." This can be a life lesson and a learned skill for you who are young, including you who are college students. Social media is so pervasive in your lives, and the demand to share your lives online is a powerful force. Many of you are savvy about creating your online image and personality. I imagine you learn most of this through trial, error, and many hard failures about what not to share online.

When you're in middle school and post something online for the whole school to see, the next day when you show up can be interesting. Of course, with social media, once it's out there, it's out there for life. I constantly cringe about what might have been videoed had cell phones been around when I was growing up, with all my public acting out as a teenager and college student.

A Restorative Process can help you learn from your social media mistakes. It can help you become the person you want to be and learn how to present an image that represents your passions and purpose.

When my daughters were very young, and some of their friends had more access to social media and cell phones than they did, my spouse and I tried to help them learn from the experiences of their friends. We made a big deal of discussing and showing them the effects of posting on social media things that were now out there forever.

Okay, so we know that talk is cheap and that we should be careful about what we post on social media. But we still fight that urge to try to explain and defend ourselves when we make mistakes. I have a rule for myself with Facebook: "Only sports and pictures of my family." That's usually all I post. But, yes, I have broken my own rule, and yes, I have made mistakes. Immediately after I've posted something else and the first response comes in, I'm asking, "Why? Why, you idiot?" It becomes easier to stop yourself when you have a clear mission, vision, and values.

Alcohol changes the chemical makeup of your brain, and this is why it is unwise to go on social media and post after drinking, a lesson many people learn the hard way. For many older adults, social media is a new world and not something we had to navigate growing up. Teenage years are a time to experiment and to learn from your mistakes.

But now the stakes are potentially much higher. Almost everyone is walking around with video cameras in their pockets and the ability to instantly share information with the world. So a momentary act of stupidity can become an ongoing, permanent part of your story for people to see for the rest of your life, including your future employers, your future partners, and yes, even your future children. A lot of harm can be caused in an instant.

On the brighter side, our devices give us infinite amounts of comic mishaps and life bloopers to watch. And adults can help accompany young people through the challenges of living in this environment. May all young people learn sensitivity and wisdom greater than the technology they need to use it.

RESTORATIVE QUESTS

I've made a list of activities you can do—"Restorative Quests"—when you have free moments to help you become more adept at living restoratively. Try these:

Involvement

#5, page 235 in *The Restorative Practices Journal*:

Step beyond what you're comfortable doing and try something new in your community. Look for an activity that strengthens one of your self-care areas for improvement.

Pay it Forward

#8, page 235 in *The Restorative Practices Journal*:

Do a random act of kindness for a stranger. Pay for the next person in line. Can you do this without telling anyone what you did? How can you incorporate these types of activities into your daily life?

Rise and Shine Ritual

#13, page 237 in *The Restorative Practices Journal*:

Try to incorporate one healthy habit when you get up. You might set the alarm a half-hour early. Stretch for 10 minutes. Read for 10 minutes. Or sit with a cup of coffee and enjoy nature.

CHAPTER FOUR

Mentoring

"Find people who make you better."

MICHELLE OBAMA

W hen I first worked in the area of student conduct, I quickly learned that if I just kept meeting with a student once a week, I could help and guide them through their failures. Many of these students had no one they could be vulnerable with. Their relationships with their parents seemed to be surface level, and, for various reasons, they could not open up to them about their failures. Part of my job was to line up hearings, one-time meetings to adjudicate policy violations. At some point I began scheduling a meeting to meet with each of these students again the following week. My schedule quickly filled up with these weekly meetings.

My supervisor informed me that I didn't have time to meet with every student who came into my office needing help. Of course he was right, but this attention seemed to be what these students needed. These contacts made a difference. But one-on-one-conduct meetings only scratched the surface of the long-term behavior changes these students needed to make if they were to rise from their failures.

I started exploring a mentoring program. Many existing programs train volunteers to be mentors for college students, but there was limited research or ideas about what to *do* when a mentor and a student actually got together.

So what should a mentor do?

I signed up to be a mentor in one of our university programs to see what I could learn. I was sent an email with a student's name, telling me that I should start to mentor them. The only instructions I got were simply to meet with the student and do whatever I chose. I read everything I could about mentoring, but there was not much useful information available.

I began to pilot a mentoring program, assigning mentors to those students who showed a need for long-term help. But I also developed outcomes, using the existing research I had done.

At first I experimented personally with students by talking about learning from failure and setbacks, employing in these meetings many of the things I was reading about coaching one-on-one and mentoring in business. As the program became intentional and effective, I developed trainings and invited a group of mentors to work with me in helping the many students needing support.

Other mentoring programs I became aware of lacked training and merely introduced students to a mentor, hoping good things would happen. Volunteers were often reluctant to be mentors because they didn't know what to do. Instructions, goals, and processes were inadequate or unclear. The idea of mentoring "judicial offenders" tended to increase everyone's anxiety levels, making potential volunteers even more hesitant.

To deal with these concerns, I explained that the training would address all of the steps of the mentoring process. I learned that ongoing support for mentors was necessary, and that we needed to develop a space where mentors could meet to discuss practices that worked and those that didn't. My team and I stayed in touch with the mentors and checked in with them on a regular basis. Each week we sent them a list of activities they could do with their mentees. We developed an ongoing newsletter with information about what other mentors were doing and what was effective. We also showed the mentors the results and the changes that were taking place among the students, due to their work.

We required mentees to write a final reflection paper, answering specific questions about the experience and how they changed as a result. During 20 years of working in student conduct, I never saw anything close to these reflection papers in terms of positive behavior change. Mentors read firsthand the amazing effect their mentoring had on their mentees. Student conduct staff members read the effect the mentoring program had on the students they assigned to it. We also did assessments to see if the students' sense of belonging grew due to the mentoring practice. It was one of the first assessment efforts in student conduct to show a positive effect on their sense of belonging.

If you would like to find a mentor to help you through a setback, look for someone who:

- ❖ is committed to you and the process of seeing you succeed
- ❖ has some common interests with you
- ❖ can develop a trusting relationship where you both can be vulnerable, honest, and authentic
- ❖ is a good listener
- ❖ is willing to share life stories with you
- ❖ is committed to telling you hard truths with love
- ❖ will challenge you

Someone who exhibits all these traits may be hard to find. That's okay. Find the best person you can and get started. If it doesn't work out, search again until you find a better fit.

One of the first people I mentored through a Restorative experience was a 20-year-old football player. He had stolen some CDs out of a car and was caught by the police. He was sent through the college conduct system, and, because I had played football in college, my supervisor thought I would be a good match to meet with him. It was his last chance. If he didn't change, he was going to lose his scholarship, be kicked out of school, and maybe end up in jail. He was the first mentee, and I was the first mentor, in this pilot program.

As we prepared to try out the idea, we had setbacks, failures, and times when we thought the process required too much work, that we wouldn't get adequate funding, and that people didn't want to change anyway.

But when I began working with an actual person who needed to change his behavior, my motivation to succeed and get better notched up to a high level. If you create something but never start doing it, if you wait until everything is perfect, you may wait forever.

The student definitely did not want to be there and was out of his comfort zone. We started our relationship on common ground: football. I loved hearing about his experiences and how the university team was doing, and he loved hearing about the old days when I played (or at least he humored me and said he did). We talked about many things and got to know each other on a deeper level. We eventually talked about the incident that got him charged with theft. He was required to meet with me for 16 weeks, the length of a college semester.

Fifteen years have passed, and we are still good friends. He is married with two daughters of his own and is coaching football. He has mentored countless athletes over the years, who have grown into strong, resilient citizens. He serves his community, his church, and the university where he currently works. We will never know what his life would have been like if he had been charged criminally, expelled from the university, and had lost his scholarship. I know that he paid back the harm he caused. He took care of his obligations so he could graduate from college, and continues to engage and serve others today.

Discovering your support people

Finding your Restorative Community can be a powerful experience and a step towards long-term growth in life. You may already have friends, relatives, mentors, or people you admire and respect, but intentionally looking for people who you can share your failures with, and who are willing to give you the truth with love, will honestly change your life. I have found that people want to help and support you and are usually honored when you ask.

I have a painting above my desk at work which one of my favorite graduate students created. It is a picture of mountains with the sun rising through them and the quote, "We Rise By Lifting Others." This inspires me, and I attempt to live it every day. We grow and feel connected by helping and supporting others—and this restores our communities. Finding your support people, and then sharing this Restorative Process with them, is a gift for both of you. Take time to welcome your support people and encourage them to share their stories of overcoming adversity.

By engaging in the Restorative Process and joining a Restorative Community, we acknowledge our brokenness, accept the need for help, show strength and courage by sharing, and give our time to others. This creates a cycle of restoration. We model to the world a better way to live in community, how to be accountable, and the transformative power of sharing.

Choosing a mentor

Choosing a mentor to work with you through the Restorative Process is a good place to start building your support network. There is no perfect mentor or right way to do this. As you work through the Restorative Process, it may be necessary to try, fail, and try again. It may take a while to find the mentor who works best with you—someone who is a good listener, has the time to commit to supporting and meeting with you, and who cares about you.

What to look for in a Small Group participant, and next steps

Finding a group of people who are willing to share together and who each have similar qualities as a mentor (see page 94) may not be easy, but we've learned that "perfection is the enemy of the good" (Voltaire). The key is finding a group of people who are committed, motivated, willing to share themselves, and willing to work at helping others.

A Small Group does not have a magic number of people. Three or more is a good place to start. The more people who have committed, the more challenging it usually is to find times when everyone can meet.

Find a special space for your meetings. Doing Restorative work is different from our normal interactions. We are vulnerable, sharing emotions, telling stories of our failures, and getting to the deeper roots of issues. This is hard to do in a public place like a coffee shop. It is important to find a space where all of you are comfortable.

Sitting in a circle with no barriers between you creates an ideal setting for sharing. An open circle takes us all back to a time when community engagement involved elders and other members sitting in circles to discuss the challenges, needs, and obligations of their communities.

The setting should be private and comfortable for three or more people, with no barriers or distractions. Everyone's cell phone and other

> ### RESTORATIVE QUESTIONS
>
> *Who could you ask to work with you through The Restorative Practice Journal?*
>
> ---
>
> *What about this person makes them a good mentor for you?*

devices should be turned off so participants can focus fully on each other. This could be a time to use a talking piece (see page 76). Find an item that represents something to your group which members can pass around. Remember the rules:

❖ Whoever is holding the talking piece is the only one who may talk.

❖ Whoever is holding the talking piece should have everyone's undivided attention and respect.

❖ Anyone can pass the talking piece on without speaking, but it can come back around to you if you change your mind and want to say something.

Be sure to remind people of these rules before each Circle Process.

There is no single right way to run your Small Group. You can deviate from the Circle Process and do it another way. It helps to be flexible, take a break from the Circle Process when needed, and give grace to people who may break the Circle Process "rules."

Hard mentoring: "truth with love"

As you work toward finding a Restorative Mentor or Restorative Small Group, and as you become more comfortable discussing the ups and downs of your life, challenge yourself to find someone who will give you honest feedback about your faults.

Caution: This might be an extremely difficult thing to do while you are in the middle of a setback or failure. Many people are very uncomfortable giving and receiving negative or critical feedback. So find someone you trust and know well enough that their feedback will make you stronger. Tell them specifically that you want and value their perspective, and that you are doing this to make yourself better. Explain that you would like them to talk with you about your negative qualities, how you are perceived by others, and any blind spots you are not aware of.

If they say they can't think of any faults, you may want to invite someone else. Or you might want to ask your original choice to think about your request for a few days, and then meet somewhere comfortable where you can discuss it again. Maybe buy them a cup of coffee.

If they have never done this before, suggest that they give you feedback in small doses, such as one critical comment followed by two positive ones.

The point is, this practice can change your life. Having people who can tell you firmly but gently how you come across, and what your blind spots are, can give you an advantage that most people don't have. When you find someone who can give you this type of feedback, hold on to them because they are a true friend. Who do you know who you can ask to give you the truth with love?

Creating a culture and spaces where you can share and intentionally reflect on failures and setbacks is not easy. It is counter to the current culture, but the effort to do this will pay off tremendously for you and the people you care about.

We have discovered three different, yet effective, ways to reflect on and process your setbacks as you experience life with others:

- ❖ One-on-one Restorative Mentoring
- ❖ Small Restorative Groups
- ❖ The self-guided *Restorative Practices Journal*

> ## RESTORATIVE QUESTIONS
>
> *Who are some people* who could form a Small Group to work through *The Restorative Practices Journal* together with you?
>
> _____
>
> *What about each* of these people makes them good candidates?

Since it is extremely hard to share our struggles and failures, the key is to start with a trusting relationship. Finding the right process, person, or group is essential so that you can express your authentic self and have support in making meaning of your failures. Since Adam and Eve in the Bible, people have been ashamed of their mistakes and have attempted to hide and bury them. Breaking this process starts with having the courage to open yourself up to another person.

One-on-One Restorative Mentoring: Work through *The Restorative Practices Journal* with someone you can share feedback openly and honestly with. Challenge each other's thinking. Be your authentic selves. Share the truth with love. Meet regularly and discuss the questions asked in the *Journal*.

Small Restorative Group: Find a group of people who can share openly and honestly with each other. Have enough people to offer a variety of perspectives, challenge each other in different ways, help hold you accountable, and be respectful, supportive, and encouraging of each other.

Find the right number of people who can commit to meeting regularly, to being their authentic selves in a group, and to taking the time to commit to the process. A Restorative Small Group uses Restorative Practices to create the best type of environment for authentic sharing and digging deeper to examine life's struggles.

Self-guided *Restorative Practices Journal (see pages 136-254)*: Take time to share your inner self-talk and examine your struggles. The practice of putting things down in writing can be very powerful. Start using the *Journal* by yourself. Then, when appropriate, share your *Journal* reflections with your Mentor or Small Group. There is no one correct way to work through *The Restorative Journal*. Like life, experimenting, taking risks, and reflecting on what does and doesn't work is how we find out what is best for us in our environment. The primary goal for working through *The Restorative Journal* is to grow your ability to respond to setbacks and failures.

Each of these three different processes can help challenge and support your Restorative Process in different ways. Each requires vulnerability, accountability, and commitment to others. Do one method alone, or combine two or three together to see what works best for you.

If you work with a Restorative Group, you have the opportunity to compound your growth and wisdom by learning from both your own setbacks and failures and from those of others. This is challenging and takes risk, but the benefits are worth it. The time and effort you put into cultivating your Restorative Community will be well spent. Today there are many options to engage with people online and from a distance. You can work through any of the three processes in online formats if you wish.

The key is to begin! Choose a process to begin using *The Restorative Practices Journal.*

There is no single correct way to rise stronger from setbacks and failures. How we as individuals respond to setbacks and failures, we often learn early on from our families and others we are close to. That behavior is then met by a culture that does not like to talk about such occurrences and shames individuals who fail. Using a Restorative Process to guide you through the *Journal* will increase your resiliency, hold you accountable, and help you rise stronger from your setback.

What way of journaling feels most natural to you? Writing by hand? Entering what you're thinking on a computer or other device? Doing an audio recording? In Restorative fashion, you can start one way and switch to another, experimenting to see what works best for you. If you have never used a journal before, it can be intimidating. The key is to be comfortable with the way you put down your authentic thoughts and feelings.

Sharing your story with a trusted mentor

Coming together to share your Restorative story is powerful. It reinforces accountability and growing as important outcomes to rising stronger. Flipping the story from making excuses, blaming others, and stretching the truth, to one of sharing your honest story with someone you trust, can create a real impact. *The Restorative Journal* (beginning on page 136) will help you record your story. If you're honest in what you write, you will eventually discover meaning in the way in which the many small stories fit into your life. The behaviors you chose that led to your failure are only the start of your Restorative story, not the ending.

Sharing with others about what you have experienced and learned after the setback is another aspect of the process. The process of rising stronger begins with reflecting on your story, and then sharing what you've learned since your setback. This changes your self-talk from "I am a failure" to "I failed but I'm still here. In fact, I have learned, grown, and changed because of this experience and have risen stronger. I am accountable, I am courageous, and I want to serve others by sharing my story."

Many of my personal failures came as a result of the choices I made involving alcohol. In one incident during my freshman year of college, I was at a party and drinking heavily. I remember dancing with a girl in the kitchen of a house. At some point the residents of the house decided that their party had been taken over by the football team, and they were unhappy that we were dancing with their girlfriends and drinking their beer. Suddenly someone was grabbing me and telling me I had to get out. They were attempting to kick out anyone that was on the football team.

I was pulled outside, a brawl broke out, and I was being held by one of the house residents as the police arrived. I tried to break free, which worsened the situation. A police officer grabbed me and threw me on top of the police car. A short wrestling match ensued. I was quickly cuffed and put in the back of the cop car. It seemed the officer chose to make an example out of me, and I could hear him yelling, "Time to leave unless you want to join your friend in the back of the car."

I felt myself sobering up very quickly. A few of my friends made attempts to plead with the officer to let me go. But when he asked them if they had been drinking or if they wanted to join me, they walked away. So there I sat, on my way to spend the night in a small-town jail.

Spending the night in jail is not a fun experience, nor is it supposed to be. It is designed to be cold, scary, and sobering. I remember getting out of jail the next day and walking back to campus broken, ashamed, tired, and sick to my stomach. My friends all wanted to hear my story, yet we were all afraid of the football coaches and university officials finding out. The older players told me to do everything I could not to let them find out. I also did not want my parents to know what happened.

My football player friends all seemed to think the story was funny, and I took on almost legendary status for my role in the "fight" and taking one for the team. I never talked about the shame I felt, the fear I experienced in jail, and my worry about possibly losing my college education. Inside my head my self-talk was, "Well, dummy, you are a screw-up in college just like in high school."

When sharing my story with others, I left out my negative thoughts and perceptions of myself. I also did not correct my friend's fabrication that I knocked the guy out and fought with a police officer. I was drunk and some details were hazy, but none of that happened. I never told the whole story or my thoughts afterward to anyone who potentially could have helped me learn, grow, and rise stronger from the experience.

My parents found out what happened when the criminal charge letter was sent to my home address. That led to an extremely unpleasant phone call with my mother. The discussion with the attorney was about how I could mitigate the damages as much as possible, not the real story or how I was feeling. Instead, it was: "Forget accountability and truth. You do not want a record, so let's quickly get this over with and move on."

When I was called into the head coach's office, there was a lot of yelling and talk about the reputation of the football team and how this better not happen again or I was done. I do remember the coach saying I may have a problem with alcohol, and I should look into that. And that was it—back to football, school, and life.

While I didn't attempt to share the true story, or how I was feeling, with anyone after that, I did, however, hear many other people tell my story. I never bothered to correct the missing details, and the story was usually told in a humorous fashion with me as a drunken idiot—although respected for my fighting ability and defense of the football team.

> ## RESTORATIVE QUESTIONS
>
> *Who have been good* mentors to you in the past?
>
> _____
>
> *What about them* made them good mentors?
>
> _____
>
> *What did you learn* from each of them?

Because I never corrected this version of the story and never shared what I carried inside my head, I constantly reinforced my personal narrative of "You are still a little dumb punk." Better to be laughed at than pitied, I thought.

I did learn and grow from this experience, but not in the right direction. Because I listened to the narrative in my head, I became what people expected. My story of myself was never challenged, and I continued to drink, party, and play football. Over the next four years I had many similar experiences to the one I've just described. I was put in jail one more time, but, by the grace of God, I never landed in jail for an extended period.

I don't blame others for not mentoring me at that time because I wasn't ready for it. Mentoring first requires the hard work of building a trusted relationship, and then taking on the tough job of examining our screw-ups. A mentor and mentee must *both* be dedicated to giving their time to each other and to the process. Mentees must be committed to doing the work between mentor meetings, including answering the tough questions about themselves prior to meeting with their mentor.

When I met with Susan in the summer as her mentor, I explained

> ## RESTORATIVE QUOTES
>
> *"I'm somebody who finds adversity almost as good as encouragement. It's almost like, if you close the door, I'll find 10 ways to kick it in or go around it or dig under it or something."*
>
> DIANE WARREN, SONGWRITER
>
> *"When I dare to be powerful, to use my strength in the service of my vision, then it becomes less and less important whether I am afraid."*
>
> AUDRE LORDE

that I was going to tell her the hard truths, and she might not like what I have to say. She said, "That's what I want." But like most people, she found it a lot harder than she expected to hear the hard truths about herself.

Susan was really struggling during her first year of college, and her parents told her she had to stay the summer in order to "get back on track." She was not happy with the plan and really wanted to go home to New Jersey to spend the summer with her friends.

As I got to know Susan, and she started breaking down her walls and sharing her authentic self, it became clear that she had developed some very negative habits during her first year in college. She had lots of friends who partied with her, and she never told her parents what she was really doing with her time.

I met Susan one morning for coffee and told her some of the hard truths I thought she needed to hear. I had only gotten through maybe half of the information I planned to share with her when she said, "Please stop! This is too much." I realized that she had never really had anyone challenge her way of thinking or her behaviors. When you've lived your whole life this way, it can be extremely difficult when someone finally holds you accountable.

She and I decided that I would give her one "truth with love" per meeting. In between meetings she would consider what I told her and develop a plan to change. For the whole summer we worked at having her change her negative habits, while she also learned to hold herself accountable. She created a life Mission Statement, she made a list of what she valued, we met at the bookstore and picked out books to discuss together, and she decided to change her major. She came to realize that she needed to develop some new positive relationships.

It was a difficult summer for Susan, but in addition to changing her major, she ended up getting involved in positive groups on campus. She eventually graduated with honors.

Developing a Mission Statement

"Simplicity is the ultimate sophistication."

Leonardo da Vinci

One of the first activities of a mentoring program is to have your mentor help you develop a process for coming up with a life Mission Statement. Creating a Mission Statement is one way to motivate yourself to achieve your goals and conquer your current struggles. The statement helps motivate your passion and persistence for doing the day-to-day hard work.

In working with many people over the years to do this, I've found that creating a simple one- or two-sentence Mission Statement which you can memorize can be extremely powerful. Even though it's been around for quite a while, Laurie Beth Jones's mission development process in *The Path: Creating Your Mission Statement for Work and for Life* (see Suggested Reading on page 255), is quite helpful.

Here's what I've learned:

❖ The overall point is to create a statement that inspires you and which you can refer to each day as you make big and small decisions.

❖ Share your Mission Statement with people close to you and see what they think. It's a good indicator if these people say, "Yes, that describes you well." On the contrary, if they say, "This sounds really good, but it doesn't fit you," you will need to change either the direction of your life, or change your Mission Statement.

❖ Post your Mission Statement where you can see it every day. Have it be a constant reminder of what you are passionate about.

❖ Be creative, using pictures, quotes, or anything else that makes your life Mission Statement meaningful to you.

RESTORATIVE QUEST

Bookstore Hunt (#6, page 235 in *The Restorative Practices Journal*): Go with your mentor or a friend to a local bookstore and pick out three books each. Choose one book that represents your past life, one that represents your current life, and one that represents your future. Come back and share your books.

CHAPTER FIVE

Motivated to Change My Behavior

"Just when a caterpillar thought the world was over, it became a butterfly."

ZHUANG ZHOU

If we aren't motivated to actually change our behavior, theory and philosophy are just ideas. But this is where the rubber meets the road. Despite its age, *Changing for Good,* Prochaska, Norcross, and DiClemente's book, describes a helpful process, designed to start where each of us is. (See Suggested Reading, page 255.) Only when we *want* to change are we able to be guided through stages to different behavior. None of us will be motivated to change if we aren't ready to change. This applies to all of us, including the students who violate university policy and do not meet with me by choice.

How do we motivate ourselves to follow through and develop the habits necessary to change our behavior long-term? Reflecting about who we are, making meaning from what's happened, and rising stronger from our setbacks are all extremely important steps in becoming who we want to be. It is our actions every day that matter.

First, are you—or the person you're mentoring or charged with disciplining—ready to change behavior? Students who violate university policies all share one thing in common—they don't choose to meet with me. They are not motivated to change on their own. Getting a university violation is the catalyst that forces them to examine their behavior. For most of them, the problem is never their behavior, but the fact that they got caught.

Prochaska, Norcross, and DiClemente's *Stages of Change* ideas are an outstanding tool to help make sense of how motivated someone is to change. From their book come these helpful observations:

Four *Facts* about Change:

1. Change does not happen all at once. It is a process.
2. We can exert some power over the course of our lives.
3. We can change behaviors, thoughts, and feelings.
4. All change in the end is self-change.

Five *Stages* of Change:

1. Pre-contemplation: Not seeing the problem. Denial.
2. Contemplation: Seeing the problem. Considering action.
3. Preparation: Making concrete plans to act soon.
4. Action: Doing something to change.
5. Maintenance: Working to maintain change.

All of us go through each stage in this order.

Experiment. Think of something you want to change. Which stage do you think you're in?

Be honest with yourself. Remember that you will go through each stage in order. When you make a mistake, you'll need to recycle through the stages, going back to the Precontemplation stage and starting over. But when you go back, you can usually progress fairly quickly through the stages.

Change is a process. You may cycle through the stages many times before you actually commit to changing your behavior.

One of the keys to changing behavior for the long-term is doing the right thing at the right time. If you attempt to push ahead to a stage when you're not ready, you can make things worse.

The Restorative Practices Journal includes experiential and behavioral exercises you can use to move yourself along in your change process. Practice the different Actions and determine what works best for you. You may need to try a number of different exercises as you go through the different stages of change.

> ## RESTORATIVE QUESTIONS
>
> *Pick a behavior* you want to change and determine what stage you think you're in. Why do you think you are in that stage? What do you think could move you forward?

Motivation

"Sometimes we're tested, not to show our weaknesses, but to discover our strengths."

Unknown

What does it take for any of us to change our behavior? How do we stop just talking, make the necessary changes, and then consistently take the steps necessary to become the persons we want to be? Throughout my career, I have tried to answer these questions as they relate to 18- to 20-year-old students who need to change their behavior. The answer is motivation, what I call "The Big Mo." A big challenge is when persons don't want to change their behavior, but the university—or anyone else—says they must.

We implemented the Facts and Stages of Change way of working at behavior change into all of our processes in the university's judicial affairs system and began assessing its effectiveness. Many of the students who were required to come to my office did not think they had a problem. It was always something outside their control: "The police are out to get me." Or, "The university staff hates me." They were making excuses. The problem was never them or their behavior; the problem was they got caught. I heard so often, "But everyone else is doing it."

You simply cannot force anyone who doesn't think they have a problem to immediately take action to change their behavior. We all have to be met where we are and moved along in sequential stages before we can take action ourselves and change. There is no one single way to motivate a person to change. What works for me does not always work for you.

Experiment with and practice the various techniques in *The Restorative Practices Journal* (pages 136-254) to see what works for you. I observe that for some students, getting caught once, and learning they will be suspended if it happens again, is enough motivation for them to take immediate action and change their behavior. For other students, getting into trouble multiple times, being arrested and spending the night in jail, and learning that they will be jailed for a longer term if it happens again, does nothing to change their behavior long-term. The motivation just isn't there—yet.

Only when we become honest with ourselves and determine that we need to change, will we take the first step toward making lasting behavior changes.

Are you curious about where you—or someone else—might be, as far as changing your behavior? Simply ask, "What is your plan to change your behavior?" Most of us have not thought about this question before. Why would we have a plan to change what we're doing when we don't think we have a problem?

The Five Stages of Change ideas have helped me realize that when you tell someone they have to change, but you don't recognize if they're ready to change, you create more resistance. Simply put, telling someone that they need to change when they don't think they have a problem makes them angry. The same is true for yourself.

For the past 20 years at the university where I've been on staff, I have worked on, discussed, brainstormed, and mostly banged my head against the wall trying to successfully address the issue of alcohol abuse.

When we assessed the effectiveness of our process and educational programs in changing behavior related to alcohol use, we made some interesting discoveries. At first the results looked awful. Students' behaviors were getting worse after meeting with an administrator and going through an educational alcohol program.

When we analyzed the results, we learned something fascinating about the Stages of Change idea and our students. Students take their pre-test about their readiness to change while waiting in the Judicial Affairs office, right *before* meeting with the hearing officer. These students have been charged some time prior to this meeting, possibly spending the night in jail. They've gone through the criminal process, and then waited to find out if they were considered "responsible" through this university process, and what their sanction might be. Pre-test results for most students showed that they were far along in the Stages of Change and well on their way to changing their behavior.

We gave them the post-test *after* they went through a meeting with a hearing officer, had completed an alcohol education program, received a strike on their record, were put on probation, and were told their parents had been notified.

The post-test results showed they had slipped back, as far as being ready to change their behavior.

The valuable lesson we learned is that during the Five Stages of Change, an individual cycles through those stages an average of five or more times before actually making long-term behavior changes.

When students take the pre-test, they report that they will never drink alcohol again. They have spent the night in jail, gone through the court system, and are getting ready to face the university judicial system. They are scared, and so they tell us they will never drink again. But after the student leaves our office, their experiences with jail and the judicial hearing fade to the backs of their minds. They join their friends at parties, have "just one drink," and eventually seem to forget all the past negative experiences and consequences.

What I have seen is that they usually start with, "I'll just go to the party with my friends and have one beer." Guess what! The police don't come storming out of the bushes and arrest them, they don't go back to court, and they don't get charged through the university system for that night out with friends drinking one beer.

RESTORATIVE QUESTS

Motivation playlist

#9, page 236 in *The Restorative Practices Journal*:

Make a playlist of the top five or 10 songs that you find most motivational. Listen to the playlist when you need a push forward.

Picture/Vision Board

#10, page 236 in *The Restorative Practices Journal*:

Create a poster with pictures that represent your top values or pictures that represent your mission or vision.

Time marches on, and one beer turns to two. Going out just on Saturday turns to Thursday, Friday, *and* Saturday. Before long, they have the same drinking habits they had prior to getting into trouble. Typically, they stumble back to their residence extremely late on a Thursday night after consuming 10 beers, when a police officer spots them and asks if they're okay. At that point, all that's happened before comes rushing back to the front of their brains. "Oh, crap," they think, "I'm going to be in big trouble."

Now it's too late. Fast-forward, and they go back through all the negative consequences and experiences that eventually leads them again to my office. The students who told me six months ago they were never going to drink again report that they were drinking as often and as much as they were drinking before.

What happened? They had a plan that they were never going to drink again, or at least until they turned 21. Are they motivated *now* to do what they need to so they actually *change* their drinking behavior? It depends on the person. Some have lost their jobs, their families, and their freedom because of alcohol or drugs.

Motivation is the key to making changes in our lives, to really doing something different, to developing new habits, and ultimately becoming the persons we want to be.

Discovering what motivates you to change your behavior is absolutely necessary when you want to deal with your setbacks and failures. Review the Five Stages of Change (pages 109-110) to determine how really motivated you are to move forward. Do this openly and honestly, ideally with your Mentor or Small Group. Are you

---

RESTORATIVE QUOTE

"The secret of change is to focus all of your energy not on fighting the old, but on building the new."

Dan Millman

still making excuses? Do you still think the problem is the environment you're in? Until you take responsibility and are accountable for your failure, you can't successfully begin to work through the Stages of Change process.

Part of my responsibility as a college administrator was addressing student behavior. I always started by asking the student to tell me the story of the incident that led to their being charged. One case exemplifies what occurred on a regular basis, often near the beginning of a new school year.

A freshman I'll call Will was disrupting his community as he came home late at night, making lots of noise and causing damage to property. Over time, Will said disturbing things to other residents about the harm he was going to cause. His behavior escalated until he came home late one night after a lot of heavy drinking and chased another student with scissors.

At this point, Will was threatened with expulsion from the university. But he showed up for his appointment with me, along with an entourage of "supporters."

It turns out that this conduct was not the norm for Will. He was academically gifted and a pre-med major who had never been in trouble during high school. Will came from a very wealthy family and had attended an elite private school. His dad was an affluent attorney, as were his sister and uncle. Will arrived with his group of attorneys to "fight" this case to ensure that he continued his enrollment.

Over many years of addressing similar behavior and students like Will, I found it useful to start such meetings by attempting to create a space where the truth could be told and feelings and emotions could be expressed. This was often difficult to do when a student came in with a prepared "story" of the events that brought them into my office.

Setting up a space for a truthful story to be shared seemed unlikely to happen in Will's case. The meeting started with his entire family and so many accompanying attorneys that we had to meet in a conference room. What normally starts as a conversation began with what was very close to a court proceeding, led by Will's father. He maintained that the university was not going to disrupt Will's future over these silly incidents that had been exaggerated, and that poor Will was a victim of people in the hall bullying him into this behavior. While the father, uncle, and sister attorneys presented Will's case, I looked at Will who sat with his head hung low, never making eye contact. Through years of experience I learned to trust my gut in these situations, knowing that there was more to this than the family was presenting. I felt Will wanted to tell his story; his behaviors were uncharacteristic, so there must be a reason for them.

As Will's sister summed up her final arguments about why Will was facing a terrible injustice and why the university would be making a big mistake if they pursued this course of action, I thanked everyone for their time and said I would like to meet with Will alone. Will's uncle forcefully objected. Since this was not a court of law, and criminal procedures are not part of what we do, Will's dad argued, too, that Will was not in a place to meet with me alone, and he refused to allow it to happen.

Finally I looked at Will and said, "I would like to talk with you alone and hear your story." As Will's sister started to stand and strenuously object, Will spoke for the first time and agreed to meet alone. Will's family and team of attorneys tried to talk him out of this course of action, but Will was firm and said it was okay. Will's father encouraged him not to say anything, and Will's sister said she would like to come in with him. I firmly stated again that I would like to meet with Will alone.

We walked across the hall into my office and sat down together. I sat at my desk. Will sank down into a couch across from me. I sat and looked at Will for what seemed like forever. It took me many years to get comfortable with this type of silence, but I had come to see the power in it. I sat staring at Will until finally he broke the silence.

"You see, Dr. Bacon, it all started. . ." Through tears, Will shared that he had never done anything like this before, and that it was totally out of character for him. Will admitted to everything that was in the report I had in front of me. While continuing to sob, he said that he did not want to be at this university and major in business. He wanted to go to college back home and major in theater.

It was clear to me, from listening to many stories like Will's, that he was afraid to tell his family this. After my brief experience with his family, I could tell why. As Will finished his story, I said I would like to call his dad into my office and have him repeat what he just told me.

Will did not want to do this. He said, "There's no way. You met my dad. He will kill me." This was part of the challenge and support process, and I knew it was going to be a huge undertaking for Will. I reminded him that I would be right there with him, but he needed to be honest with his dad. After this discussion, Will agreed, and I stepped outside to get his father.

However, Will's sister was sitting right outside my door listening. She had a very pale and serious look on her face but did not say a word as I walked into the conference room and addressed Will's father. "Will would like to talk to you." We walked back into my office and sat down. It took Will a few minutes to gather himself, and then, through tears, he

---

RESTORATIVE QUOTES

"Strength doesn't come from what you can do. It comes from overcoming the things you once thought you couldn't."

Rikki Rogers

"Champions keep playing until they get it right."

Billie Jean King

"We may encounter many defeats, but we must not be defeated."

Maya Angelou

explained to his dad that everything was true. He had done all these things, and the truth was that he wanted to go home. He never wanted to be here, and he didn't want to major in business.

When Will was finished, his father got up without saying a word and walked out of the room. He grabbed his sister and Will's uncle and said, "We are leaving." Will was left on the couch with his head in his hands, sobbing. I comforted him and reminded him of the truth he had told.

Although Will thought his life was over, that his dad would kill him, and that he had no future, none of it was true. He made it through a tough situation. I agreed with him that it was not going to be easy and that the road ahead would likely be difficult. But he was here. He had come this far. I reminded Will that he had options unlike many students facing felony criminal charges who were going to spend time in jail. This was not the case for Will.

Will's future was in his hands. He could take control of what he did from this point forward. I had just watched him show tremendous courage as he shared his truth with his dad. As we parted, Will shook my hand and left. I don't know what happened between Will and his family after that day. He withdrew from the university, and I never heard from him again. Before the meeting, I had been talking with Will's family at least four times a day, but after that meeting they were never in touch.

I learned from my experience with Will, and from many students in similar situations, that intervention and programs will not help someone change their behavior if they don't think they have a problem. We had attempted to get Will to stop his bad habits immediately and start doing things differently. But none of us had taken time to really understand him and why he was doing what he was doing. Will's alcohol abuse and negative behavior actually were helping him reach his goal of not being at the university. The more we threatened, sanctioned, and educated, the more resistant and defiant he became.

Many of our current systems and cultures do not allow sharing or seeking the truth. Instead, we have a culture that starts with excuses—blaming other people, circumstances, the way we were raised, and so on.

If an individual seeks legal "counsel" to go through the criminal process, the truth seems to be quickly displaced by a concerted effort to get out of trouble, to mitigate the consequences, to find technicalities, or to tell another version of the "truth." I have witnessed many students becoming caught up in these responses to their transgressions. They become passive observers, watching others get them out of any real consequences. This does not lead them to change their behavior and learn from the experience.

I have found through many meetings with students that, in the end, they *want* to tell the truth, even when the consequences could be severe, even when their counsel is telling them, "Don't say a word to the Dean of Students," or when they themselves say, "I have been advised by counsel not to answer that question."

They want connection and engagement, particularly with someone they can trust, with whom they can break down and be their authentic selves. Such an exchange cannot begin with a lie. A one-on-one mentor relationship can often be the best place to create space for truth-telling and being one's authentic vulnerable self. This type of association and environment can set the stage for examining current behavior and supporting someone through a change process.

The Restorative Practices Journal will help you create a detailed, specific plan to change your negative behavior.

If you don't think you have a problem, is there something you could do to start contemplating if you might need to make a change?

Have you ever created a plan related to what you want to change? There are days where you will not feel motivated, but those are the days where you need to be disciplined. It is during the long grind back when we learn what we are really capable of.

RESTORATIVE QUESTS

Storm Chaser

#35, page 245 in *The Restorative Practices Journal*:

How can you stretch yourself, take a risk, or do something outside your comfort zone this week?

Quotes

#36, page 245 in *The Restorative Practices Journal*:

Collect quotes that inspire, push, or help you rise stronger. Where can you post these quotes to help inspire you, create passion, or help you persist?

Books

#37, page 245 in *The Restorative Practices Journal*:

Collect books that can help you make meaning from your setback or failure. Collect books about people who inspire you.

CHAPTER 6

Self-Care

"Things that hurt, instruct."

BENJAMIN FRANKLIN

Immediately after facing a setback or failure, we need self-care. This can be challenging because we're often feeling sorry for ourselves, and feeling shame.

Developing awareness of what you need, along with habits of self-care, are essential for long-term success. A Mentor or Small Group can assist you in seeing the importance of self-care during difficult times. Whatever the setback you experienced, taking care of your basic and immediate needs is vital. Eating and sleeping well, and assessing your living situation, are extremely important.

Using a setback to reevaluate your self-care habits is one way to change yourself for the better. Doing this will give you some confidence that you have control over at least parts of your life. You can take action immediately, and the effects of these changes can help restore you, prepare you for the work of examining your life, and rise stronger.

If you have a Restorative Mentor or Small Group, invite them to work with you to develop a plan of self-care. This could include exercising together, shopping together for healthy foods, picking out and reading books together, and doing something simple like going for a walk and talking about life. When you have someone with experience and wisdom assisting you, they can help you examine any blind spots you have related to self-care.

When you are at your lowest point from a failure, doing something very minor to help you feel good about yourself, to feel accomplished, is the beginning of rising stronger. Working out at the gym, washing your car on a sunny day, and having coffee with a friend are all examples of good first steps. When you do healthy activities and volunteer to help others, you're also taking care of your own health, with the added benefit of feeling good about helping someone else.

As part of a Restorative Small Group you can do many activities together—start a fitness group and work out together, swap recipes for healthy cooking, share information about various self-care opportunities in your area, and serve a community need together. The key is to hold each other accountable to following through with your plans.

We often focus on just one or two areas, when there are multiple areas of wellness that need attention. Take some time to examine how you take care of yourself, and learn to practice self-care in a variety of ways.

Ongoing self-care opportunities are often available in your local community or online community. Explore resources and opportunities in all areas of wellness.

Failures and setbacks give you an opportunity to discover new ways of living better. You gain wisdom. When you apply that to your self-care needs, you will grow as a full person, "actualize" yourself, and become the best person you can be. People who are wise and successful have learned that they have to take care of their best asset, themselves. You cannot chop as many trees with a dull axe, and you cannot be excellent if you are not at your best.

Self-awareness

The first step in self-care is self-awareness. If you have never thought intentionally about caring for yourself, seek a Mentor or a Small Group, or ask someone who is good at self-care, to help you. Remember, this is more than physical wellness. Restorative self-care means addressing all aspects of self-care. Not just physical wellness. If you have focused to an extremely high degree on taking care of one area, you have probably let other areas go.

As a high school and college football player, there were times when I dedicated a large part of my life to getting physically better. I focused on my strength, speed, and conditioning to improve my football abilities. College athletes can spend so much time consumed by this one area that they fail to recognize the many other

---

RESTORATIVE QUESTIONS AND ACTIONS

To begin, pick one of the Seven Areas of Wellness shown in the circle on the facing page, and on pages 186-194.

❖ List all the **harm** you think you have done to yourself in this area.

❖ List all the **needs** you have in this area of wellness.

❖ What **obligations** do you have to others in this area, which, if you took care of them, would improve your own self-care?

Make a list of the actions you want to take to meet the needs and obligations you've listed above. Make a plan for how you will do that. What can you engage in right now to improve your self-care in this area?

areas of wellness in life where they need to succeed. *All* of the wellness areas affect your performance as a football player.

During my college football career, using the knowledge I had at the time, I did everything to improve myself physically to perform on the field. That meant getting up early to lift weights, run sprints, and do conditioning drills. I was dedicated in the off-season to making myself better, and it showed when the season came around.

I spent no time preparing my mental capacities and leadership abilities. I never talked to anyone about being a leader for my teammates, or read books about leadership and how to make others around me better.

What I love about football is that it requires a full team effort to be successful. There are always 10 other guys on the field who need to be doing their jobs for the team to do its best. By focusing exclusively on making myself the best I could be, I left motivating and leading my teammates to dedicate themselves to our common goal by the wayside. Years later when I started to study leadership, I realized how limited my knowledge and experience were.

RESTORATIVE QUOTES

"You gain strength, courage, and confidence by every experience in which you really stop to look fear in the face. You are able to say to yourself, 'I lived through this horror. I can take the next thing that comes along.'"

Eleanor Roosevelt

"We don't ever know how strong we are until we are forced to bring that hidden strength forward. In times of tragedy, of war, of necessity, people do amazing things. The human capacity for survival and renewal is awesome."

Isabel Allende

Since I still love the sport of football and work regularly with college athletes, I share my story because I now understand the importance of strength in all areas of your life. I enjoy giving college athletes books to read about leadership. I believe this practice of sharing my story and giving back to athletes has helped me grow and overcome my anger of not winning as many games as I would have liked.

When speaking to a college football team before the season begins, I start by asking them to raise their hands if they want to be undefeated. Everyone's hands always go up, as they should before the season starts. Everyone should be optimistic and confident. I imagine every program across the country feels this pre-season confidence.

Then I ask how many of them want to win the division, and how many want to go to the championship game. Again, everyone's hands go up.

Next I turn to individual goals. How many people want to be starters? Usually most, if not all, hands go up, even though they all know that only so many players can start in a given year. Everyone at this point in the season is confident and thinks they have a chance.

Then I ask how many of them want to be all-conference and how many want to play beyond college? Fewer and fewer hands go up as we go through the questions, but there are still always a lot of hands, even when I ask how many want to go to the NFL. Few players are likely to make it to the NFL, particularly from division IA football, but with the exuberance of youth, many still think they have a chance of realizing their childhood dream.

Now I make a big switch and ask them to raise their hands if they are doing everything in their power to make all their team and individual goals a

RESTORATIVE QUOTE

"Give me six hours to chop down a tree, and I will spend the first four hours sharpening the axe."

ABRAHAM LINCOLN

reality. Their coaches are in the room when I do this, so all their hands go up. I start asking them very specific questions about how they use their time. "Keep your hand up if you never missed a workout this summer. If you never missed a weightlifting session all summer." Hands start going down very quickly.

When I ask how many of them play video games, all of their hands go up. I tell them I did, too, and back in the day, no one could beat me at Atari video football. I ask how many spend hours a day playing video games, and most of their hands are still up. I ask how playing video games helps them reach all the team and individual goals they just told me they had.

I remind them that they didn't say they wanted to be normal or average. They said they wanted to win the division and some wanted to go to the NFL. So I ask, "How is playing two hours or more of video games a day helping you achieve these high goals?" I ask, "Did you read a leadership book this summer that will help you be a better player in the upcoming season, and also be a better leader?" Usually no hands go up. I ask, "Have you sat down with someone who is where you want to go, like the NFL, and asked what they needed to do to get there?" Usually no hands go up.

If you want to be great champions competing at the highest level, why are you not doing everything in your power to reach those goals? I get into the details: Do you go to class to remain eligible? Sit in the front row? Strive for the dean's list? Introduce yourself to your professors after class? Meet with your professors during office hours? All these steps help you reach the goals you have for yourself.

Many students aren't doing the little things to become great because they don't know what it takes to be great, or to obtain the unbelievably high goals they've set for themselves. They may know what

> **RESTORATIVE QUOTE**
>
> *"I am not what happened to me. I am what I choose to become."*
>
> EMMA WATSON

it takes to make their *bodies* stronger and faster, but rarely have they thought about what type of *character* is needed for a team to win the division, or what type of *leadership* is needed throughout a long season.

Remember to start with what you know. For many of us, that's how to take care of ourselves physically. And then seek help to adapt that discipline to *all* areas of wellness. Adapting the hard work you've used in one area to another can become a formula for success, which you can apply to all of life.

When I started to focus on learning, I used the formula I had for success on the football field—to hustle! I was never the biggest, strongest, or fastest player on the football team, but no one was going to out-hustle me. The off-season was my time to improve and work harder than everybody else. I was the first at practice and the last to leave. Likewise, realizing I was not the smartest person in the classroom, I had to hustle more than my fellow students to be successful academically.

Whenever my three daughters complain about something related to sports or ask for advice about sports, I tell them only one thing: "Work harder." Translating this mentality and habits to academics helped me succeed.

When I tell people from my past that I am a Dean of Students and have a Ph.D., it takes them a moment to catch their breaths—if they don't pass out from shock! They remember the guy who never opened a book and spent a lot of time engaging in unproductive activities during high school and college.

One of the biggest challenges in my Ph.D. program was the Statistics requirement. Long before I began the class, my self-talk was that I was no good at math, as illustrated by my undergraduate accounting coursework. I still assumed they didn't let guys like me get Ph.D.s. This Statistics class was where they would finally weed me out. The course was as hard as I expected it would be.

But now I had some wisdom and applied my successful football practice to my classroom learning. I worked harder and smarter. I hustled! I found a professor who knew that not all students were mathematicians, but they still needed to succeed in Statistics to get their Ph.D. I out-hustled everybody in that class, took full advantage of the extra help during the professor's office hours, and arranged study groups to learn from other students.

In the end I squeaked by with a hard-fought B. I was prouder of that B than any A I ever got, because that grade represented change, growth, and perhaps a little wisdom.

This accomplishment was a turning point in my self-talk, indicating that I was growing, becoming more wise, and could deserve one day to be called Dr. Bacon. I have met with many of you who have struggled academically, and I have a formula and a story to share with you. It is powerful for any of us to meet someone who overcame academic and personal struggles, and failures, to become a Dean of Students with a Ph.D. I want all of you to know that I turned it around with hard work, perseverance, and hustle, and so can you. Take hope for your own restoration. You can become mentally stronger and more prepared for pursuing the greatness you desire.

Many of us have blind spots, concentrating on some areas of wellness while ignoring others. It is important to share openly and honestly with someone you trust to truly examine all areas of well-being. *The Restorative Practices*

RESTORATIVE QUESTIONS

What can I do to take care of my physical health today?

_____

What books can I read to grow intellectually?

_____

What is one thing I can start doing today to improve my financial situation?

_____

What can I do to grow spiritually today?

_____

Do I need to seek professional help to meet my emotional needs?

_____

What one thing can I start doing to improve my relationship with the environment?

Journal examines all seven areas of wellness, including assessing current practices and making plans for improvement.

Like everyone, I fail regularly, and in some areas of my life I don't spend the time I should to learn, grow, and conquer my challenges. I occasionally use avoidance and excuses to deflect responsibility for rising stronger.

True freedom depends on us taking control of our inner voices and mastering ourselves. I know from experience that I need to do the tough work and take small steps to challenge and stretch myself. I need to be willing to be uncomfortable and, at times, scared.

We live in a country that values freedom above all other rights, and we don't have some of the limits to freedom that affect other parts of the world. But our own blind spots and unwillingness to work through our challenges can keep us from being truly free. Finding strategies and developing a plan to practice self-care should be a lifelong practice.

RESTORATIVE QUESTS

Negative to positive

#31, see page 243 in *The Restorative Practices Journal*:

Let this be your mantra for the week. Look for a negative situation in your life and figure out a way to turn it into a positive situation as you're able.

Two birds, one stone

#32, see page 244 in *The Restorative Practices Journal*:

Let this be your mantra for another week. Look for opportunities to get two things done during the time you would normally get only one done. Or create two successes out of one opportunity.

CHAPTER 7

Challenge and Support

*"Only the best fall, so they can
pick themselves back up."*

—Alfred Pennyworth, from "Batman"

The balance between challenging yourself and supporting yourself is a lifelong endeavor. Sometimes when you're going through, or recovering from, a storm in your life, you need more support. As you grow wiser and stronger you need to be able to stretch and challenge yourself.

Writing down your experiences of challenging yourself, sharing those experiences, and, then holding yourself accountable for taking action, are important aspects of the process. Doing these steps with a trusted Restorative Mentor, Restorative Small Group, or Online Restorative Community can help you actually implement these challenges and engage with your support systems.

If you're not challenging yourself, you may not be growing. If you're not failing and not experiencing any setbacks, you may not be challenging yourself enough. If your goals and dreams do not scare you, you may not be dreaming big enough. The growth process requires us to challenge ourselves—reasonably—and attempt to meet those challenges.

Having support does not eliminate the potential for failure, but it does significantly reduce the likelihood of failure breaking us or putting us in an unsafe situation.

"Unsafe" is on a continuum. How much risk you are willing to take will determine how safe you are. I don't think the main goal in life is to be safe. Albert Einstein said, "A ship in harbor is safe, but that is not what ships are built for."

Having a Restorative Mentor or a Restorative Small Group to challenge and hold you accountable can also be a good support network when you're playing it safe. If a group of people are all aware of the challenges each one is going through and sharing them openly, they can all grow together. Even when you're not with your Small Group, just knowing they are in your corner, supporting you and waiting for you to share your story, is helpful.

Going through the Restorative Process helps you create a balance between challenge and support as you learn the Process. It can also help you learn how to challenge and support yourself in the future.

I have a niece who had a good chance of swimming in the Olympics in Tokyo. If she made the team, I had promised to fly our whole family to watch and cheer her on. That was a strong motivation for me to conquer my fear of flying because I really wanted to support her in this amazing opportunity. Since the Olympics were in Japan, one of the longest possible flights from the United States, it may have been too much challenge for my first flight.

RESTORATIVE QUOTES

"Unless you try to do something beyond what you have already mastered, you will never grow."

RALPH WALDO EMERSON

"I cheer for people . . . I was raised to believe there's enough sun for everybody."

TRACEE ELLIS ROSS

This opportunity motivated me to take intermediate steps by pursuing programs that would help me manage my anxiety about flying, including starting with a shorter flight. Challenging myself and getting some small wins was an important step prior to taking a long flight to Japan.

You will have to find the balance between challenge and support with any given growth opportunity you face. When you want to change your attitudes, behaviors, or habits, you need to balance the support you need to make this change with the challenges you use to push your growth.

You can use *The Restorative Practices Journal* to share your challenge and support chart (see pages 184-186) with your Restorative Mentor, Small Group, or Online Restorative Community. Since it is important to give yourself rewards when facing challenges, your supportive Restorative Mentor or Small Group can cheer for and reward you—as you'll do in turn for them.

Self-actualization is not about playing it safe. If you haven't failed recently, or struggled, you probably haven't challenged yourself enough. Experiencing the Restorative Process and Seven Practices will give you the confidence to stretch yourself and take on the numerous challenges in your life.

You can readily find examples of the challenge and support balance in movies. Harry Potter had the immense test of facing the Dark Lord Voldemort, but he had the support of his mentor Dumbledore and his two best friends. Luke Skywalker had the challenge to save the universe from the Evil Empire, but he had the support of his mentor Obi-Wan Kenobi and his band of rebels. America's first president, George Washington, faced the gargantuan challenge of fighting the British Empire. He had the support of his fellow patriots, but they knew they also needed the support of France and Spain.

These three examples illustrate that support often comes from people helping to share the burden of our trials. When facing the storms, think of the people in your life and what support they give you. We can begin to intentionally foster more supportive relationships and also learn to eliminate less supportive relationships. The value of having supportive people in your life is never more evident than when you face struggles and challenges.

RESTORATIVE QUESTS

Workout Challenge

#15, page 238 in *The Restorative Practices Journal*:

Find an exercise or physical activity you have never done before and try it. Do it with a friend or group.

Meditate

#16, page 238 in *The Restorative Practices Journal*:

Try meditation. Check online to watch an introductory video.

New Challenge

#25, page 241 in *The Restorative Practices Journal*:

Find a place in your community you've never been to. Visit there with an open mind.

Play Time

#27, page 242 in *The Restorative Practices Journal*:

Pick a game or purposeless activity you enjoy. Maybe a simple card game like rummy. The point is to do something just for mindless fun. It can often be more fun when you do it with others.

PART 2

THE RESTORATIVE
PRACTICES
JOURNAL

CHAPTER 1

Before You Begin with
The Restorative Practices Journal

"In a gentle way, you can shake the world."

GANDHI

There is no one correct way to use *The Restorative Practices Journal*. Some things may work for you and others may not. I suggest that you pick at least one of four ways to help you reflect, grow, and share while going through the Restorative Process:

1. **Work alone with *The Restorative Practices Journal*:** Jump in and get going after you've read this overview. Actions begin on page 168.

    Share with other people if and when you're ready.

2. **Work with a Restorative Mentor:** You can choose a mentor to walk with you on your journey. Find someone you trust, so together you can share your deeper inner thoughts and feelings. If you can, find

someone who has used *The Restorative Practices Journal* themselves. The key is to have someone you can open up to. You want them to tell you the hard truths with love, be there during the storms in your life, stay in the fire with you, and help you reflect on the experience and make meaning from it. Part of this process is going to be uncomfortable, and that is okay—and worth it!

If you've been through all of this already, consider becoming a mentor.

3. **Work with a Restorative Small Group:** Pick a group of people who are open to reflecting and examining the mistakes they have made, are willing to hold each other accountable, and are capable of speaking truth to you and to each other. A Small Group can be extremely powerful because you have different people looking at your setbacks and life, and offering a diverse, rich perspective that you by yourself, or you with only a mentor, cannot.

4. **Work with an Online Restorative Community:** You can invite persons from a distance to support you and hold you accountable by leveraging all the various online ways to communicate and share. Connect via Zoom, email, text, or even through snail mail. Experiment and find what works best for you and those who are participating.

In whatever way you decide to use the *Journal*, remember that one of the key components to developing resiliency and rising stronger is sharing. Holding things in, listening only to your own self-talk, and having no one to challenge your thinking is not the best way to learn and grow. You will need a combination of challenge and support to change. Find people who will support you, push your existing way of thinking, and motivate you to do the difficult work that you need to learn and grow.

This *Journal* includes a form of the word *"Practice"* in its title for a reason. It's to remind you to experiment, make mistakes, and create a process that works for you.

There are Actions here for you to practice yourself—or to suggest to others you're coaching.

Practice is a day-to-day grind. It is hard work, messy, and imperfect. But practice is where we all develop, learn, grow, and build the strong roots to prepare ourselves for upcoming storms. May we all learn to value our practice time and stay committed to the journey.

Life is tough. You are tougher!

Restorative culture embraces struggles, screw-ups, setbacks, and failures as opportunities to learn, grow, and rise stronger. We want to share our struggles and setbacks so we can learn and grow stronger together. The ancient Greek philosopher Socrates said: *"The unexamined life is not worth living."*

Through this Restorative journey we will address our current screw-ups and ways of working with any struggle or failure we may face during the rest of our lives. This is how we grow in wisdom and take the necessary action to apply the wisdom.

Struggle and failure can lead us to doubt ourselves and feel paralyzed from moving forward. This *Journal* includes steps for examining our challenges, discovering the meaning behind our struggles, developing healthy habits, taking care of ourselves in times of struggle, and transforming ourselves into the people we want to be.

We are each on a lifelong journey filled with challenges. This *Restorative Journal* is part of our support and growth process. The best programs in the country on growing students' resilience demonstrate the critical need to share our setbacks. We

> **RESTORATIVE QUOTE**
>
> *"We all rise by lifting others."*
>
> Robert Ingersoll

may think everyone else in the world is thriving except ourselves, but that's not true. Everyone is struggling and has screwed up.

Make *The Restorative Practices Journal* your own

If you're struggling from a recent screw-up or failure, no matter how big or how small, you are welcome here. We have all been there, and we know that if we continue to stretch ourselves and take risks, we will struggle again. Let's not fear the upcoming storms we will encounter, but embrace them as the opportunities they are.

"Fate whispers to the warrior, 'You cannot withstand the storm...' The warrior whispers back, 'I am the storm.'"

Be you, unapologetically, ready to challenge and support yourself.

There is no one right way to rise stronger from your setbacks. Everyone deals with life's struggles in different ways. Here are some of the basics involved in using the *Journal* as part of the Restorative Process:

Work through the *Journal* at your own pace.

If you wish, skip whole parts altogether. Come back to them at a later time if you want.

Add Activities, questions, and things to do, if you want.

Use this *Journal* to mentor someone you care about.

> *Find a method for keeping this Journal that works best for you. Maybe you write in a separate clean journal. Or make electronic notes that you can keep and share.*
>
> *Whatever you choose, keep it close or handy so you can make notes whenever an idea or thought, memory or question comes to you that you don't want to forget.*
>
> *You will grow and progress. You want to keep a record of all you'll be learning.*

You may want to work on a single practice for a whole week. Other times you may want to do multiple practices in a given week.

You can choose a Restorative Quest to do in between journaling or meetings with your Mentor, Small Group, or Online Restorative Community.

You might want to pick a trusting- and relationship-building Activity to do during each meeting.

Check your mental health on a regular basis to see if you need help from others.

There may be some practices or processes that don't fit you or what you are going through. Feel free to skip them.

The Restorative Practices Journal comes from research, theory, and evidence-based practices about how to foster resiliency, grit, self-care practices, and a growth mindset. It also includes Actions to learn to motivate yourself and begin changing your behavior and self-talk, along with practices from Restorative Justice. We draw on these resources to establish a process that is unique and creates a space for people to use when they face screw-ups, struggles, setbacks, and failure.

> ## RESTORATIVE QUOTE
>
> *"If you don't stick to your values when they're being tested, they're not values. They're hobbies."*
>
> Jon Stewart

HERE'S WHERE WE'RE GOING

Here is a preview of some of the areas where we'll be working:

Your Mission Statement

Early in the Restorative Process, it will be important for you to identify and reflect on who you want to be: your identity, what you're allowing to shape you, your purpose, and your meaning in life. Very few people have a clear picture of who they want to be and what their purpose in life is. Most people start with what they want to *do* in life. Not *why* they want to do it in the first place, or *who* they want to be.

The process of creating a Mission Statement is necessary as you begin the Restorative Process. Reflecting on your setbacks in life changes you, and your mission may become clearer. Reviewing your Mission Statement at least yearly will allow you to tweak, change, and adapt it, based on your experiences and the meaning you have made from those experiences.

To make their Mission Statements memorable, some students have painted amazing pictures or created a sculpture to represent their statement. Some students get tattoos of their Mission Statements.

For a Mission Statement to succeed, you will have to think hard about who you are and what you want your life to be about. You will want to constantly reflect on what is working and what is not. Your Mission Statement must be tied to your motivation for rising from setbacks and failures.

Your values

Determining what you value in life—what is important to you, what your priorities are, what you care about, what is the best way to live, and what you're willing to do to keep following your values—is another activity you can undertake with a trusted mentor.

There is no one correct way to create your list of values. Values can be represented with one word, with statements, with examples of other people or things. It is your values that actually motivate you to take positive action and to make those actions your priority.

Making a list of what you value can help motivate you and help you live out your actions on a day-to-day basis. Keep the list of what you value in a place where you can review it daily. Values can help you evaluate your current behavior—are your actions aligned with your values?

Your vision

What would it look like if you were living out your mission and values day-to-day? A vision is a concrete plan of what you want your future to look like.

Here's a taste of what's ahead for you in the *Journal*—Imagine and write a detailed story of what a day in your life would be like if it were based on your mission and values. Your vision should inspire and motivate you to get to that place.

On page 236, Quest #10 suggests that you draw a picture or write a detailed description of your vision. You may want to create a vision board, where you post pictures that represent your future best life. Reviewing your vision, or looking at your vision board during the storms of your life, can be helpful.

Applying theory; observing my mental health

It is extremely important that as you work through *The Restorative Practices Journal,* you periodically reflect on your mental health and assess whether you need professional help. The *Journal* has questions related to your mental health throughout and suggests when you might want to talk to a professional counselor. Pay attention to those questions. But don't rely only on the questions within the *Journal.* Examine yourself for signs of depression and/or anxiety. Here are some additional questions to ask yourself or to ask the person you are mentoring:

> **RESTORATIVE QUOTE**
>
> *"Make your vision so clear that your fears become irrelevant."*
>
> KERWIN RAE

- ❖ Do I need more help with my current mental health?
- ❖ Have I been withdrawing from life? If so, how?
- ❖ Would it help me to see a counselor?
- ❖ What local counseling services are available to me?
- ❖ If I am in a mental health crisis, who can I call? What resources are available to me?
- ❖ Who can I talk to about my current mental health?
- ❖ What actions can I take to improve my mental health?

Do I have a growth mindset?

It's helpful to come into a Restorative Process believing that your abilities can be developed. But if you aren't sure about that, *The Restorative Practices Journal* will help you along. This process is about embracing struggle as an

<table>
<tr><td>

RESTORATIVE QUOTE

*"This is hard.
This is fun."*

Carol Dweck

</td></tr>
</table>

opportunity to grow stronger and wiser. Restorative leaders don't let things just happen to them. When challenging things happen, an enlightened person uses them to learn and grow.

Reframing failure

"Individuals who believe their talents can be developed through hard work, good strategies, and input from others have a growth mindset. They tend to achieve more than those with a more fixed mindset, those who believe their talents are innate gifts. This is because they worry less about looking smart, and they put more energy into learning," says Carol Dweck, a psychologist who specializes in mindsets.

Think about someone who fails a test. When they get the failing grade back, do they say, "I'm stupid and terrible at math." Or do they say, "That was tough. I haven't figured out how to do math yet." The key word when struggling with anything is "yet." Like elsewhere in the Restorative Process, it is not the failure that should be focused on. It is the self-talk after the failure that matters.

Keep these questions in mind as you work through the *Journal*:

- ❖ Do you have a fixed mindset or a growth mindset?
- ❖ How do you think that embracing a growth mindset can improve your performance?
- ❖ How can a growth mindset help you when you struggle?
- ❖ How can a growth mindset help you with your self-talk?
- ❖ Think of something you currently struggle with or have failed at. How can you reframe and describe your struggle using a growth mindset?

Preparing to grow: Restorative space for meeting with my mentor

The physical space which you create and use for your Restorative Process is extremely important. You are doing something different and difficult, and using the same spaces that you often work in may make it harder to take you to the new places you want to go.

If you meet with a Restorative Mentor, you will be sharing difficult information about yourself. Find a place that's comfortable and provides the ability to give each other undivided attention and respect. When you're talking about sensitive and personal topics, it's best to be away from others.

Preparing to grow: Restorative Small Group space

If you meet with a Restorative Small Group, you will want to have deep and personal conversations. So meet in a space that feels respectful and open to authentic sharing.

What helps you completely focus on the task at hand? What could distract you? What objects, pictures, chairs, or kind of table motivate you to speak honestly and listen carefully? Adding certain items that inspire can be helpful. Ask your group for feedback about the space you have created.

You may want to use the techniques of a Circle Process with your Small Group. A talking piece may help to structure your group's sharing. A reminder about how to use a talking piece: Only the person holding the talking piece may talk. Everyone else gives their undivided attention and respect to whoever holds the talking piece. The talking piece is passed around the circle so that everyone gets an equal chance to participate. Each participant always has the right to pass the talking piece without speaking. But as the piece continues around the circle, they may choose to speak the next time it comes to them.

How much Grit do I have?

Angela Duckworth defines grit as "perseverance and passion for long-term goals." Grit is one of the key components in determining how successful persons will ultimately be, not only in college, but in life. After getting to know the life stories and pasts of some students, I concluded they have off-the-charts grit. I told them I have no doubt that, in the long term, they will be successful, no matter what they do.

> **RESTORATIVE QUOTE**
>
> *"Enthusiasm is common. Endurance is rare."*
>
> Angela Duckworth

I remember one person, who was struggling with his classes, telling me that the electricity was turned off in his apartment because he couldn't afford to pay the power company. He casually mentioned that this was a common occurrence, but that he had a way of living with it until he could get enough funds to have the electricity turned back on. He went on to say that he sent his mother money to get his car fixed, but she used it on drugs, and now he had no car to get to his job.

After working with this person for a few years, I came to realize that he was facing challenges most people couldn't dream of, yet he constantly found a way to lift himself back up and move forward. I appreciated that he was willing to share these parts of his life. I let him know that I thought he had an unbelievably high level of grit. I had confidence he was going to do great things. This student went on to graduate school and a doctoral program. To this day, every time he calls me, I am excited because I know he has done something great.

Having a mentor or small group who can help you recognize your strengths during adverse situations can help you overcome them and build on your strengths. We all know that life is challenging, and we will all fail. Those people who have developed the trait of not letting their failures and obstacles deter them from their long-term goals are highly likely to succeed. *The Restorative Practices Journal* will help you assess your current grit level and develop a plan for growing your grit.

Encouraging yourself—Collect quotes

Collect quotes that inspire, motivate, and help you rise stronger. Post the quotes in places where you can see them every day. Post them in the spaces where you journal or meet with your mentor. These quotes can be used to help motivate and inspire you on a daily basis. I have included some of my favorite quotes throughout this book and *Journal*.

Encouraging yourself—Find books

Collect books that have helped you make meaning from your setbacks and failures. As you begin to examine your life, create a library to help you toward your stated mission. Self-help books, as well as stories of other people's recovery from failures, can assist you in rising from your own struggles. Here are a few classics that I recommend to people who are struggling:

- ❖ *Everything Happens for A Reason: Finding the True Meaning of the Events in our Lives*, by Mira Kirshenbaum.
- ❖ *The Four Agreements: A Practical Guide to Personal Freedom (A Toltec Wisdom Book)*, by Don Miguel Ruiz.
- ❖ *Cousins: Connected Through Slavery, A Black Woman and a White Woman Discover Their Past—and Each Other*, by Betty Kilby Baldwin and Phoebe Kilby.
- ❖ *The Path: Creating Your Mission Statement for Work and for Life*, by Laurie Beth Jones.

❖ *Man's Search for Meaning*, by Victor E. Frankl.

❖ *The Little Book of Restorative Justice: Revised and Updated (Justice and Peacebuilding)*, by Howard Zehr.

Consider sharing your quotes and books with your Restorative community.

How do I not repeat the same screw-up?

If you haven't done so already, ask yourself, "What exact behavior(s) do I need to change in order to prevent this type of failure in the future?" I urge you to *write* your response so you have a gauge to measure your accountability and your responsibility, and so you can show others through your actions that you have changed. You are making a commitment to yourself to no longer be the person who made the mistake.

In my experience, most students, when asked about their current misdeed, will tell you, "I am never going to do that again." And they believe it, particularly when meeting with the Dean of Students. But even in this moment of truth, they still give excuses or reasons for why the behavior occurred. They tend to make themselves appear as victims in the situation, who had no control over what they did, which led to being charged with a violation. Any of us in this situation should change our self-talk and tell our story honestly, acknowledging that we are in control of the outcome(s).

Maybe there were circumstances beyond our control that led to the incident. But ask for help from your mentor or your group to examine the entire story,

> **RESTORATIVE QUOTE**
>
> *"You could not step twice into the same rivers; for it's not the same rivers and you're not the same person."*
>
> ADAPTED FROM HERACLITUS

and then come up with ideas about what you could have done to avoid what happened. This action will give you tools to avoid negative consequences when you're confronted with similar situations in the future.

As I've said, most screw-ups made by college students involve alcohol—usually extreme amounts of alcohol. Often, their "friends" convince them to take just one or two shots with them before continuing to study.

But alcohol changes the chemical makeup of your brain. I am not saying that you go from two shots to streaking naked across the University quad. Two shots lead to making the choice to have two more shots. Those two more shots can lead to thinking, "Well, I've studied enough for the evening. I can go out for an hour to hang out with my friends. Going to a party and having one beer won't hurt anyone. I can still be home in an hour to get a good night's rest." Look at the math. You have now chosen to drink four shots and one beer. You are no longer thinking rationally. You are no longer capable of making sound choices.

From here the story usually goes something like this: "My friends were all drunk, and I didn't want to leave them at the party. But I couldn't drive home anymore because I had been drinking. I wanted to do the right thing and not drive and, at the same time, help my friends."

Whoa, stop, pause. Do the right thing? Here is where **challenge** and **support** can come in. We all need our thought process to be confronted at this point. How could you have "done the right thing" earlier in the night before the drinking commenced?

After we've been charged as responsible, given a mentor to meet with for the semester, and gone through hours of processing, we might begin to change our thought processes. Hopefully by then we will have come to a place where we hold ourselves accountable for the actions throughout the night that led to our getting in trouble. Ideally we will have reflected on why we are in college in the first place and what our mission is.

If we are living our purpose and mission, hopefully our friends and acquaintances will see that on a Thursday night, when we have an exam the next day. Your real friends wouldn't even ask you to take a shot with them. They wouldn't think of asking you to drive them to a party, because they know through your actions that you care about your education. They recognize that on Thursday nights you are studying in your room, or, better yet, in the library.

Getting to this point will probably not happen all at once. Sometimes it takes multiple failures and a lot of motivation to reach it. But this is the power of restoration, and of deeply reflecting on your failures and using them to grow stronger. Ultimately, it's about changing your day-to-day behavior so you don't repeat your failures and mistakes, leading you to becoming the person you say you want to be.

So what about those of us who are sitting at a party drunk, with no way home, surrounded by a group of friends who are more drunk than we are. Hopefully we each have someone in our lives who will help us see our true selves, acknowledge that we're already deep into a problem, and that it's our own choices that have gotten us into this difficult position. There are many ways out, but we're drunk and not thinking straight, or even recognizing that we could call an Uber or a friend for a ride.

If you're 18, in your first semester at a brand new school and in an unfamiliar environment, you may try claiming that you had no choice but to punch that guy who was bullying your friend. But the Dean isn't likely to buy it and doubts if you even believe what you're telling him. You may feel that you deserve a break because you're a good kid who's never been in trouble before, who's on the Dean's List, is majoring in finance, and volunteers at your church on weekends.

I have been on both sides of such a moment. You are not holding yourself accountable—in fact, I suspect that *no one* has ever held you accountable before. But this may be your opportunity to make major changes to your life story. Think about changing your self-talk and learning to be accountable and responsible—and helping others do the same.

This process doesn't happen instantly. For many of us, it takes time and multiple setbacks to be ready to change. We usually aren't ready to change if we still don't think we have a problem, if we're still making excuses, and if we rely on other people to make excuses for us. How could we possibly hold ourselves responsible and not think, "I need to change"?

RESTORATIVE QUESTS

(Do these during down-times or between Actions)

Ask to hear the Truth with Love (see Restorative Quest #1 on page 233):

This is a tough Quest, but if you make it a lifelong practice, it will help you grow stronger. Find someone close to you and set up a meeting. Maybe invite them to coffee or a donut (my favorite). Ask them to come to the meeting prepared to give you feedback on what you need to improve.

- ❖ How do I come across?
- ❖ What are my blind spots?
- ❖ What don't I know?
- ❖ What are people saying about me that I don't know?

Answers to these questions are extremely difficult to hear and to tell. Encourage the person you've invited to talk to be honest because you are asking for it. Consider picking multiple people in your life to talk with you in this way so you get a variety of viewpoints and perspectives from different areas of your life.

Graduation Card (Restorative Quest #23 on page 241):

Write a note to yourself about your anticipated graduation or another success event. Save this note to open on the day you achieve the milestone.

Accountability

Accountability is something I have attempted to nurture in college students, and something I have attempted to master myself. If you want to grow to be more accountable, who you go to for support can be tricky. It was only after I became a father that I began to gain some much needed wisdom in this area. Raising three daughters can be challenging.

Let me back up. We lost our first child during the first trimester of pregnancy, so making trips to the doctor for ultrasounds during subsequent pregnancies became highly anxiety-inducing. With an ultrasound, a doctor is able to let you view what is going on inside the womb and, if you're lucky, to hear the heartbeat of your unborn baby.

Even during the difficult and gut-wrenching experience of losing a child, we learned a lot. When we first thought about "starting a family," my wife, who is an uber-planner, was thinking about the best time to deliver the baby. How could we squeeze it into our already busy lives? We determined late November would best fit our work schedules, since we educators would be off anyway during the holidays. So we were delighted when we did a pregnancy test, and the doctor confirmed our due date was mid-November, "just like we planned."

You may have heard the saying, "God laughs at our plans." During a doctor's visit for an ultrasound, our perfect plan took an awful turn. Hearing the sound of a new heartbeat is amazing, particularly when it's your first child's. We had heard the heartbeat during an earlier appointment; this was just a routine check-in to see how the baby had grown. Everything was working as we had planned, and we assumed we were still right on schedule.

But at one point I could sense something was wrong. The doctor's face showed it; I could tell she was struggling to find a heartbeat. I can't remember exactly what she said to us, but we both knew our baby's heartbeat was not there, and she was not going to be born. I can hardly describe what I felt, what I saw my partner experience, and what I imagined she was going through. We were stunned. We cried together and shared the news with our close friends together.

In the beginning I wondered what was wrong with us because this never happens. It turns out it is more common than you may think; many people told us they, too, had lost a child during pregnancy. My own mother let us know for the first time that she had lost the baby during her first pregnancy. She had never told me that before. I felt the power of sharing in a deep way and the immediate understanding between people who have experienced similar losses.

As people talked with me about the loss, I realized that most of them now had a child or several children, and they seemed to be thriving. My mother went on to have three more children: my older brother, my older sister, and me. Other people were happy and raising healthy kids, and nothing seemed to be wrong with them. This discovery connected with us in a meaningful way and gave us hope. It made us realize this was not our permanent state, that we would get through the deep disappointment.

Sharing at the right time—when it is most needed—is a part of the healing process. We grew, gained hope, and healed with each story that people told us. In making meaning of this for myself, I came to understand that having a child is a miracle, an amazing moment, a blessing beyond anything I could have imagined, and certainly not to be taken for granted. From this experience my wife and I paid greater attention to people who were struggling to have children and empathized with their situation.

As we picked ourselves up and tried to get pregnant again, we were no longer strategizing about the best time to have the baby. We were instead praying that we would get pregnant and have a healthy child. As hard as losing our first child was, nothing else could have helped me understand so deeply the miracle of life and how precious it is. This was not just another step in my becoming an adult. Nor was it something I could read about and then plan every detail. A child is God's gift, a miracle, and something to accept humbly with extreme gratitude. When someone tells us they've lost the baby during pregnancy, my wife and I share our story. We connect in a very deep way. Together we all grow wiser and stronger for what the future holds.

Many people have very difficult stories about having children, some with long struggles to get pregnant, and some losing multiple children. Telling these stories to each other is powerful. When someone honors me by sharing their story, I am grateful for the show of trust. I am an infinitely better person because of having gone through this experience. I look at all our children differently because of it.

I have become more accountable about sharing with others, checking in with them, and showing empathy. The storms of our lives can make us better. Making meaning of this loss in our lives has made us stronger, drawn us closer together, and given us a perspective of appreciation that I don't believe I could have received in any other way.

Sometime after our loss, I was invited to an engagement party at a downtown art studio. I am not the sort of person who goes to an art studio, and I have never bought anything that anyone would call a piece of art. I was walking through the art gallery thinking, "How long until I can leave?" when a small painting on the wall caught my attention. It was a small picture of two circles, each of them resembling the earth, with one circle overlapping the other. Below the painting was this poem:

I longed to lift the burden of her sorrow

And yet I knew it was hers to carry

And so I walked next to her side by side.

I rested when she rested.

Cried when she cried.

And loved her more with each step of the road.

I don't know who wrote the poem or why, but it spoke to me deeply and reminded me of the loss of our unborn child. I bought my first painting that day. When I gave it to my wife, we shared a deep moment of reflection and knowing. We have gone through a loss, but we are still standing. We care more deeply about our children, we empathize with the many other people who are struggling to have a child, and, like the poem, we have grown to love each other more. The painting hangs in the entryway of our home, and it shares a special meaning for me and my partner every time we walk by it.

I don't know if any of our three daughters will go through this experience, but chances are that at least one of them will. I know now that we have made meaning from what happened to us, and if they do experience it, I am ready to tell our story. In fact, we will share it long before they get pregnant.

It is helpful to find someone who understands what you are going through and will share their own stories, even if those stories aren't the same. The key is that they are willing to share.

I strongly believe that it is the failures and storms of our lives that define us, make us who we are supposed to be, and help us fulfill our destiny. It is only through reflection and examining our failures and storms that we can use them to grow stronger and wiser. Going through the Restorative Process offers us tools to face the many storms ahead of us so that we can make meaning of our life stories.

None of us looks forward to failure and struggle, but when they inevitably come, do your best to welcome them like friends. Take the opportunity to use the situations to learn and grow. Learn to control what you can. Remind yourself—this doesn't need to scare me, I've prepared for surprises, I'm ready for this, I have survived similar situations before, it is not going to break me, and it will, in fact, make me stronger and wiser. So let's go!

Learning to hear your self-talk

As events are happening and you're interacting in your world, you're telling yourself the story about what is going on, about what you see, and about your behavior. You are the lead character in your story. Think about this—

❖ Does your inner voice respect yourself? Empower yourself? Support yourself?

❖ Do you notice if you ever give yourself a break?

❖ How do you show grace for yourself?

These questions aren't easy. We're used to feeling sorry for ourselves, making excuses, and blaming others for what happens to us. We often tell ourselves to forget about whatever bothers us and move on. We insist that we want to get to a place of moving forward. But it is important to want to move forward stronger and as a wiser person. A setback is an opportunity to dig deeper and examine our life stories.

No matter how small the setback or failure is, what would it take for me to see this setback as a blessing? This is hard work and not natural, but this is part of being restorative and rising stronger.

Having a mindset that uses setbacks and failures to grow stronger is what a wise person does. This is a habit and practice you can build so that eventually you can share with trusted others—I am enlightened, and anything that happens, good or bad, I am going to use to become the person I say I want to be. I am willing to take more risks and to stretch myself, because I can use whatever happens from this for good and for improving myself and others.

I have told you about my lifelong self-talk, with its overall theme that I'm a "little dumb screw-up," an imposter who doesn't belong in the position I hold. I don't know if anyone ever recognized this in me until I practiced the Restorative Process myself and began to share from within. Most people become very good at hiding their insecurities and compensating for them.

A powerful experience of sharing in college helped me reframe my lifelong self-talk. The guys I hung out with in college were just like me: young, dumb, football players, who got into a lot of trouble. But there was a moment when we told each other what our fathers said to us when we made a mistake growing up. One friend said he was called "shit for brains." Another said "dumb shit." I said that mine was "shithead." We all had a good laugh at these stories, but for the first time I realized, it wasn't just me. Growing up, I thought I was the only "shithead." But people I know, love, and trust experienced the same thing. Upon reflection, I realized that occasionally I would call one of my three daughters "manure head" when she screwed up. Some habits are tough to break, and I rationalized that at least I didn't curse at her.

But my dad's nickname for me, and my own self-talk followed me for years in my head.

To say, "This is not who I am," is hard to break. By all of society's measurements and standards, a guy with a Ph.D., serving as Dean of Students at a prestigious institution, is not a shithead. I've grown easier on myself, but I still struggle to check myself when I "jokingly" say to my students, "I am the dumbest person with a Ph.D. in the world." And I really check myself when I'm just about ready to call one of my smart and competent daughters "manure head."

This is hard work that takes time.

I want to share a common conversation I've had over the years with college students who've been arrested for selling drugs. My relationship with these students begins in a jail cell, generally at 8:00 a.m. the morning after they have been arrested—often a Sunday morning. There are many things I would rather be doing on a Sunday morning, but I realize this is a powerful and important moment in this person's young life, and I have the experience and wisdom to help.

Usually these students start by telling me, "But I'm not a drug dealer!" They are adamant about this, and they share their story of why, despite the fact that I am meeting them in jail for the charge of felony drug disruptions, they are not a drug dealer. They explain they are not a common drug dealer on the street; they were merely facilitating a transaction for a friend. They had bought a small amount of marijuana (when it was illegal) and were passing it along to a friend who gave them a small amount of money.

> **RESTORATIVE QUOTE**
>
> *"Every saint has a past, and every sinner has a future."*
>
> Oscar Wilde

It is important to hold them accountable right off the bat and tell them that what they just told me is the definition of drug-dealing. Holding them to the fire and leaning into this moment is important, made quite powerful by the fact that the Dean of Students from their college is sitting with them in jail, telling them they are charged with dealing drugs. This moment, this picture in time, is potent and persuasive.

It is an important part of their process in realizing how far off-track this moment is from where they hoped to be, where their parents thought they would be, and from where most college students are on a Sunday morning. They may be a 3.0 GPA business major who is part of the university quidditch team, and yet here they are in the downtown jail charged with dealing drugs.

The reality of their current circumstances needs to be imprinted in their memories so it becomes part of their long-term story and journey to recovery.

A week or so later I meet with the student again, this time in my office. They are still trying to convince everyone—their parents, the police, their friends, and me—that they are not a drug dealer. I remind them of the time we spent in jail together and what we talked about: "What you do from this point forward will show me, your parents, the police, and the world that you are not a drug dealer. Just repeating over and over that you are not a drug dealer won't reflect that change."

It is important to hold them accountable, including charging them with a drug violation, so they can do everything in their power—for the rest of their lives—to show themselves and others, "I am not a drug dealer."

When they seem to be at a low point with no hope of recovery, I tell them, "I've met with many students before in your exact same situation, too many. One day—you might not believe this now—but you will be glad you got caught and were arrested."

They look at me with dull and angry eyes that say, "You have got to be kidding me. The Dean has lost his mind!"

Generally, students in this situation are not big-time sellers. They're accommodating their friends or trying to make a few bucks to supply their own habit. I tell them, "Imagine that you didn't get caught that night and continued to sell drugs. Your practice might kill someone. You might get involved with the wrong kind of drug dealer and get killed yourself. You might drop out of school. The point is—what you were doing needed to stop. You needed a smack to get you back to being who you say you are: a 3.0 GPA business major who plays on the quidditch team. How can you not be thankful that this is what took you back to that?"

They may or may not believe me at the time, but one day they will. May they come to understand this moment in their life story as the time when they switched from going down one path to going down another. This is why I love my work and the Restorative Process. I can be a part of a moment in someone's life story which makes a tremendously positive difference in who they grow up to be.

I often say, "This can be your 'Now what?' moment. I'm not here to help you make excuses or get you out of trouble. There are probably people in your life already doing that for you—sometimes for a long time—which might contribute to why we are here in the first place. I am here to walk with you and to help you make meaning, to change, and to use this experience to become the type of person you say you want to be."

The farther down the wrong path you are, the steeper and harder the drop that is needed to help you take another path. I share with students, "My biggest fear is that you actually think I gave you a break. I don't want you to think at some point in the future that what's just happened was no big deal, that you didn't face any real consequences, and as time goes by, you return to selling drugs.

"You need to remember this experience, including meeting with me and crying in a jail cell. You need to remember the real fear that you might have to go to prison. Some of you may need to actually spend a little more time in jail."

The motivation to change behavior is different for every person. Often well-meaning parents and attorneys are trying to get their child or client released from the consequences and right back to life. Consequences can be motivators to change future behavior.

Keep remembering life's Three Big Questions

❖ Who am I?
❖ Why am I here?
❖ Where am I going?

The answers to these questions will change, particularly if you answer them first when you are young and going through new experiences. By the time you get to college you are away from your family and hometown, some of you for the first time. Or you might be joining the military, moving out of home, going to another town to live, or starting your first job.

The experience of failure can be an opportunity to grow. Yes, there is negativity, shame, and awkwardness about discussing it, but collectively, your life setbacks change you. Use them to move forward, reflect, and examine how they have re-formed you and the trajectory of your life.

- ❖ How have your answers to life's Three Big Questions changed since your setback?
- ❖ How do these questions help you face the storms of your life?

Engagement

Connecting my past behaviors to my future service helped me heal, make amends, gave my past behaviors meaning, and connected my old self to my new self. This was the reason for reflecting on all my past failures and setbacks. I could reframe what they meant in my life and how they did not make me a loser. They made me strong and much more prepared for my future service and profession.

My first job after finishing my undergraduate degree was working in a live-in home with troubled youths in Washington, D.C. This was the last stop, the last chance for most of the kids who had been kicked out of every other school. This group home included a day program and a residential night program. My duties included living

> **RESTORATIVE QUOTE**
>
> *"Never die easy."*
>
> WALTER PAYTON

in a room in the dorm with kids ages three to 12. In the morning I wakened my group of 10- to 12-year-old boys, got them ready for school, and had breakfast with them. Then I was off during the day. At three o'clock I returned and started our night program, engaging the kids in activities, recreation, games, and so on. We had dinner together, and I read them a book before they went to bed.

It sounded like a dream job. When I started, I still had the mindset of what's in it for me. I was living free in Washington, D.C. I received free breakfast and dinner five days a week, and Mrs. Jackson made the best waffles and fried chicken I ever ate. I was off during the day and thought I was being paid to play with kids. I always liked being around kids, so I assumed it would be easy. But from the day I started, the job challenged me, frustrated me, woke me up, and changed me dramatically. The boys I was assigned to work with came from broken families and other very difficult circumstances. Some had experienced extremely traumatic upbringings. Initially I just played and lived with the kids, but eventually their past trauma came out in their behavior.

One day when we were playing soccer outside, one of the kids seemed to just snap. He started yelling at another boy and eventually a fight broke out. I had to use the restraining techniques we were taught to stop him; then I sent him upstairs to his room for a time out. After about 10 minutes, I went upstairs to check on him to discuss his behavior.

When I got to the boy's room, he wasn't there. I could hear a strange panting coming from the bathroom area. When I walked in, he was naked and smearing feces on the wall. The smeared feces spelled out "fuck Josh." Nothing in my life prepared me for this moment. Having your name in lights is something many people dream of, but your name in feces is a big shock.

I started telling him he was in big trouble, and then he came at me with a look that said, "I'm going to kill you." He started hysterically swinging his fist at me and screaming. He was a big kid, and I didn't understand why he was so upset, particularly with me. I was attempting to use the restraining techniques

I was taught to keep from getting feces on myself. He was covered in his own feces, tears streaming down his face. His screaming turned to words I could finally understand: "Why, Mom? Why, Mom? Why didn't I stop it? Why didn't I stop it?" He crumbled in my arms and sobbed deeply.

I am not a counselor, and at age 21, I had no idea what was going on. But intuitively I knew something much deeper was happening for him. I held him in my arms and told him it was going to be okay. I eventually calmed him down and told him to go shower and get ready for bed. I didn't want any of the other kids to see any of this, so I cleaned the feces off the wall and everywhere else in the bathroom.

In hindsight this experience helped me, challenged me, and confused me. No question—it engaged me. I cared deeply for this kid, and his pain hurt me. I truly wanted to understand what had happened and how I could help him.

The next day I reviewed his file. He came from a very poor family in Southeast Washington, D.C. When he was eight years old, he witnessed his mom kill his grandfather with a knife. During the incident, he was in the other room with headphones on and came out to see his mom stabbing his grandfather repeatedly. In his young mind, trying to make sense of a scene that cannot be made sense of, he blamed himself. He thought that if he hadn't been listening to music so loudly in his room, he could have stopped his mom. His mom was now in prison, his grandfather was dead, and his dad had never been in his life. He was being raised by his grandma.

From that point forward, this kid and I started having much deeper conversations about his life, his mom, his dad, and the extreme anger that he carried with him. This experience challenged me and made me want to be a better person. It was the first time I regretted that I didn't demand more of myself during college. I wasted all those years in classes when I could have learned something that might have helped me support this kid. I felt selfish and ashamed. Fortunately, this fueled a new desire in me to learn and be better.

I bought a book to help me better understand this kid's issues and how I could help him. That book led to another book. I started having conversations with my supervisor about what was going on with these kids and how to help them grow and change. For the first time, I started to reflect on the past traumas and mistakes in my own life and tried to think of how I got through them. This was truly the beginning of an awakening, of becoming a lifelong learner, and of developing a growth mindset. The experience of helping and living with these youths from very difficult backgrounds helped me engage in life more fully. I was all in, and I now had the passion and persistence that led me to becoming someone who is here to serve others.

I would spend the next 20 years buying self-help books, biographies, histories, philosophy books, anything that I thought could help me grow and apply to helping others. This is when I decided to go back to college and learn more. My story changed from, "College was a waste of time," to "My undergraduate years were just the beginning of my college experience."

It is never too late to change and to add to your life story. I was beginning what would become a lifetime of service and helping others. I earned a Master's in Education Administration and a Ph.D. in Educational Administration with a focus on higher education and a cognate in law. I would eventually work as a case manager for the division of mental retardation in Sussex County, Delaware.

I often wondered what would have changed and shaken me and my football buddies out of our negative habits? I believe the Restorative Process, a strong mentor, and a support group could have made the difference. I had many coaches who I respected and interacted with daily, but the focus was always football and helping me improve my ability to play football.

Having someone actually take an interest in our *lives*—and not just in our ability to play football better—answers the question about what could have changed me and my college friends and motivated us to change our behavior.

We needed someone we respected and trusted who could show us another way, challenge our existing way of thinking, and motivate us to be better.

In part, this type of thinking led me to start a mentoring program for students who violate university policies. It involves a long-term intervention, with trained mentors going through an intentional process with weekly one-on-one meetings with their mentees.

I no longer wonder about the value of my college experience. I am accountable for everything I did, and I believe that God had a plan to use my negative experiences for eventual good. I looked up to my coaches as if they were fathers, meaning I feared them but also respected them, whatever they said. What if they had spent time getting to know the real me, challenging my existing thinking, actions, and behavior?

I am not blaming the coaches. Instead, I'm thinking about what I could have done. What if I had gone to one of the coaches I respected and talked with him, told him my story, opened up, and shared with him? At that age I was terribly shy and would never have dreamed of going to talk to anyone in authority. I use this failure of mine in college to better understand the students I work with now.

> ### RESTORATIVE QUOTE
>
> *"If you judge people, you have no time to love them."*
>
> MOTHER TERESA

I can use the wisdom I've gained to create a program that challenges students by requiring each of them to meet with a mentor for a semester. In the mentoring program, trained mentors use intentional steps to create trusting relationships and help each student create a life Mission Statement, along with short-term and long-term goals. The mentors are ultimately trained to help students use their failures to learn, grow, and rise stronger.

I am using some of the same habits that I started after the feces-smearing incident to help me serve students today. In making meaning of the experiences in my life, the "fuck Josh in shit" one is better than ever having my name on a marquee or in lights. It is part of my story and has helped to shape the service I have chosen in life. As I sit here and write, I have a self-help book I'm reading on the bookshelf in my office and another one on the coffee table in our living room. This from someone who used to proudly say, "I never read a book in college."

Sharing our stories is a big part of the Restorative process, and, at the university where I work, we are attempting to change the culture regarding our responses to setbacks and failures.

Serving

After you've worked through *The Restorative Practices Journal* and shared your growth story, you can become a Restorative Mentor or facilitate a Restorative Small Group. You can use the wisdom you have gained, showing others how your setback has led to growth and changed who you are. You have put your failure in perspective, you have made yourself accountable to others, you have used your setback to examine who you want to be, and committed to share and give back.

- ❖ Who can you help or give back to (maybe connected to your failure or setback)?
- ❖ Who can you reach out to and share your Restorative Story with?
- ❖ On what social media platforms can you share your Restorative Story?

The Restorative Practices Journal ends with a self-assessment. Examining yourself and making meaning are ongoing life practices. Asking yourself, or someone you care about, these questions is the ongoing work you need to do to continue to be the person you say you want to be. No matter how much any of us grow, we will continue to struggle, fail, and face storms.

We need to constantly go back to the Seven Practices (see pages 21-24, and 26-133) and use them in our everyday lives. We need to find and cultivate our own support people so we have help in sustaining these lifelong practices. We should also find and cultivate relationships where we can be the support person for someone else going through a storm.

Now What?

◆ ◆ ◆

27 ACTIONS TO GO DEEPER

You can do the following Action sessions over several weeks or weekends, or during an intensive couple of days. Some ideas include work to be completed on your own and then shared with your Restorative Mentor or your Restorative Small Group. You can also journal about any of the sessions when they're over. Finding the time and space to commit to these Actions is important.

ACTION ONE:

TELLING YOUR RESTORATIVE STORY

A major part of the Restorative process is storytelling. A Restorative Story is about how an experience changed you. It includes telling what happened, your honest reflections about what was going on, how you made amends, and then the positive outcome of the story.

Your first major action in the *Journal* is to write about your present struggle or screw-up. You don't have to be a great writer or an amazing orator to do this. But telling your story by writing is a powerful part of the process. The incident itself that led to the "failure" will likely not change, but your story will—from something that happened to you, to something that led you to grow and learn.

Put it down in writing. When you're writing your story for yourself, it's easier to tell the truth and be accountable—and to leave out the excuses and the blame we can be tempted to include when we tell our stories to others.

Free-write, brainstorming anything you want to about what happened, writing continuously to encourage one idea leading to another. The intent is to get your thoughts down and to be open and honest with yourself. Be detailed and include your feelings—both during and since your setback.

By examining your story, sharing it with others, and reflecting on your story, you will learn and grow from your Restorative experience. Ultimately, the story you compose becomes a part of who you are, showing how this setback fits into your life story.

How you tell your story will likely change from when you begin the Restorative Process to when you have worked through it. Observing how it has changed will likely give you a sense of your growth and how you have become wiser and stronger.

How you integrate and make meaning of what happened, and how the story fits into your overall life story and identity, will change. This struggle is a part of you. You're still standing, and you're now ready to take on something even bigger. Put in writing—on a screen or on paper—what happened.

Don't censor your initial thoughts. Let your pen or keyboard flow. In your own words, tell the story of your struggle, the storm you faced, a failure, or setback you are currently going through or just went through.

Tell your story honestly, but also be as creative as you want to be. Some of the prompts below may help you get started.

Question Prompts:

1. What happened that led to your setback or failure?

2. How did you feel right after the setback?

3. What did you say about yourself after the failure or setback? What was your self-talk?

4. What harm did you experience because of your setback?

5. What harm was caused to others by your setback?

6. What did you do to take care of yourself after the setback? Did you use any resources to help you recover?

7. What did you do to make things right, or as right as possible, as a result of your failure?

8. What have you learned about yourself in the process?

9. How have you grown because of the experience?

10. Was there anything you changed about yourself, your habits, or your behavior because of the setback?

Now that you've outlined or written your Restorative Story, do you see signs of growth and rising stronger in it?

Continue until you've put down all that you have to say.

ACTION TWO:

WHO WILL SUPPORT ME ON MY RESTORATIVE JOURNEY?

Review pages 92-105.

❖ Who can mentor me through the Restorative Process?

❖ Who might work with me on *The Restorative Practices Journal*?

❖ Who could join me in a Restorative Small Group?

❖ Set a meeting to discuss the process with your potential mentor or Small Group participants. Develop a plan and set meeting times.

❖ Do I want to be part of an Online Restorative Community? What trusted friends or advisors do I have who would be helpful to me?

Share your Restorative Story with your Restorative Mentor, Small Group, or Online Restorative Community. Don't clean it up. Let your raw memories and feelings stand.

When you have a moment, or some extra energy, consider doing the following:

Restorative Quest: Pick one from pages 232-246.

Restorative Trust-Building and Relationship-Building activities: Pick one from pages 247-254.

MENTAL HEALTH CHECK-IN:

As you go through the process of rising from your setback and digging deeper into root causes, it is important to know the limitations of this process and when you may need more support. Recognizing and taking the steps to seek professional counseling is a sign of strength and courage. You need to continually take stock of your mental state and seek support if needed.

Am I depressed or anxious?

_____

Have I been withdrawing from life? If so, in what ways?

_____

Would my Mentor or a trusted family member urge me to seek professional help?

_____

Ask them to help me create a plan to seek further help.

ACTION THREE:

SELF-TALK/REAL TALK

Understanding Self-Talk

How aware are you of the ongoing dialogue in your head? It's been there your entire life, but do you hear it?

Your inner voice is how you make meaning of both the events going on around you, and also of your behavior in response to those events.

RESTORATIVE QUOTE

"We become what we think about."

EARL NIGHTINGALE

This partly explains why the same thing can happen to two people and their reactions can be completely different. Past experiences influence your current self-talk.

If you've never examined your self-talk, keep a log in your *Journal* of what you say to yourself throughout the day and the week. Noticing how things affect you and how you make meaning of them through your self-talk can be a powerful, at times frightening, shocking, and, hopefully, an enlightening, experience.

As you think about your current setback, what have you been saying about, or to, yourself since it happened. Most of us accept certain self-talk that we would never accept if someone else said it to us. We tend to be hard on ourselves.

Our years of self-talk shape who we are and how we view ourselves. It ultimately leads to how we operate in the world. Over time this self-talk may become, "I'm an idiot," "I'm stupid," and other put-downs. By reinforcing that dialogue over many years, you come to view yourself this way, and that affects your choices and your decisions about taking on risk and trying new things.

If you think you are stupid and a failure, you will act that way. If this is your constant dialogue, what you have been telling yourself through the years, you will reinforce it with every new event in your life. No matter how much others whom you respect tell you that you are smart or great or successful, it is not enough to counter your own bombardment of negative self-talk.

How do you stop negative self-talk? First, you have to be aware of it. Then you have to honestly and openly examine it. Writing it down and keeping track of it is a good place to start.

Now that you're aware of what you're saying to yourself, you can share with others how you want to change it, reshape it, and create an inner voice that empowers you, strengthens you, and leads you to be the best version of yourself.

Working with a counselor to explore your self-talk can be helpful, too, since much of our self-talk stems from our childhoods.

Your thoughts are the source of your emotions and moods. The conversations you have with yourself can be destructive or beneficial. They influence how you feel about yourself and how you respond to events in your life. Take a minute and think about what you've said to yourself so far today.

- ❖ Was what you said critical?
- ❖ Was it judgmental? Or was it kind and helpful?
- ❖ Is this the way you would talk to someone else you cared about?
- ❖ How did you feel after you engaged in this inner discussion?

Self-Talk related to your struggle(s) or setback

Jot down honest answers to as many of the following questions as you can. If any feel too hard, skip over them and continue on. Come back to them later when you're ready.

Or try answering and see what you discover about what you think but hadn't consciously brought to mind.

1. What have you thought about yourself since your setback happened?

2. How respectful are you to yourself?

3. How much do you forgive yourself in your self-talk?

4. Are you lying to yourself about anything?

5. Are you making excuses for yourself?

6. Is your self-talk challenging you in a good way?

7. What other person could you share your self-talk with, and be completely honest and vulnerable with them?

8. If you could change how you talk to yourself, what would you say differently?

9. How could changing your self-talk change your life, how you think about yourself, and the actions you take?

10. How can you work on changing your self-talk so that it supports you in becoming the person you say you want to be?

11. List some positive self-talk you can start saying to yourself.

12. What am I angry about because of a recent setback?

13. Name all the "What If's" or "If Only's" you have thought of since this setback.

14. Why do I care so much about impressing people?

15. What is the hardest choice I am avoiding?

16. Do I rule my fears, or do they rule me?

17. How do today's struggles reveal my character?

See if you can create some positive mantras or statements that you say to yourself every time negative self-talk begins in your head.

When you have a moment, or some extra energy, consider doing the following:

Restorative Quest: Pick a different activity this time (see pages 232-246).

Restorative Trust-Building and Relationship-Building activity:
Pick a different activity this time (see pages 247-254).

ACTION FOUR:

A RESTORATIVE APPROACH TO THE HARMS I'VE CAUSED

The pillars of Restorative Justice are:

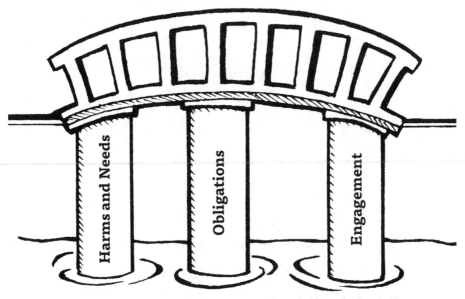

© by Howard Zehr. Used by permission.

Look at your current struggle, setback, or failure, and examine it using a Restorative lens. If you don't have a present struggle, setback, or failure, think of one from the past. Engaging in this process, and sharing this process with others, can have a healing Restorative effect.

In order to be accountable, you are attempting to make things as right as possible from this point forward. It is a proactive approach to control what you can, rather than ruminating on the past and what you cannot change. Look for the opportunity to learn, grow, and make things right.

❖　What harms did I cause to myself? (List them)

❖　What harms did I cause to others? (List them)

Reflect on these harms. Then share your responses with your Restorative Mentor, Restorative Small Group, or Online Restorative Community.

When you have a moment, or some extra energy, consider doing the following:

Restorative Quest: Pick a different activity this time (see pages 232-246).

Restorative Trust-Building and Relationship-Building activity: Pick a different activity this time (see pages 247-254).

ACTION FIVE:

A RESTORATIVE APPROACH TO THE NEEDS I'VE CREATED

RESTORATIVE QUOTE

"I know well that the greater and more beautiful the work is, the more terrible will be the storms that rage against it."

Maria Faustina Kowalska

Think of the harmed parties. If you can, ask them what needs they have that you should make as right as possible. If you can't contact them directly, you may have to imagine how others have been affected by your screw-up, struggle, setback, or failure.

List their names and their specific needs.

ACTION SIX:

A RESTORATIVE APPROACH TO THE OBLIGATIONS I NOW HAVE

Obligations are the actions you will commit to going forward to make things as right as possible.

❖   What obligations do I have to make right the harm I caused?

❖ List of obligations I have to myself:

❖ List of obligations I have to others:

List of the actions I will do to make things right, and the timetable for doing each action:

Obligation	Action	When I will begin

The Support I Need:

Reflect and share with your Restorative Mentor, Restorative Small Group, or your Online Restorative Community, about the Harms, Needs, and Obligations you must take care of. Ask for their wisdom and support as you work to make things as right as possible.

Is there someone else I should share this with to hold myself accountable?

_____

ACTION SEVEN:

LIVING RESTORATIVELY

RESTORATIVE QUOTE

"The heart of man is very much like the sea; it has its storms, it has its tides, and in its depths, it has its pearls, too."

Vincent van Gogh

Absorb the Restorative Justice Habits below. Then schedule a meeting with someone who you would like to talk with about how you can live more responsibly.

Restorative Justice is a way to deal with conflict and struggle. Howard Zehr, one of the pioneers of Restorative Justice, describes 10 ways to live restoratively.

Restorative Justice Habits

by Howard Zehr

1. Take relationships seriously. Imagine yourself as part of an interconnected web of people, institutions, and the environment.
2. Try to be aware of the impact—potential as well as actual—of your actions on others and the environment.
3. When your actions negatively impact others, take responsibility by acknowledging and seeking to repair the harm—even when you could probably get away with avoiding or denying it.
4. Treat everyone respectfully, even those you don't expect to encounter again, even those you feel don't deserve it, even those who have harmed or offended you or others.

5. As much as possible, involve those affected by a decision you will be making in the decision-making process.

6. View the conflicts and harms in your life as opportunities.

7. Listen deeply and compassionately to others, seeking to understand even if you don't agree with them. (Think about who you want to be, rather than just being right.)

8. Engage in dialogue with others, even when what is being said is difficult. Remain open to learning from them and the encounter.

9. Be cautious about imposing your "truths" and views on other people and situations.

10. Sensitively confront everyday injustices including sexism, racism, and classism.

© by Howard Zehr. Used by permission.

Answer and then discuss these questions with your Restorative Mentor, Restorative Small Group, or Online Restorative Community, or put down your own thinking in your *Journal*:

❖ How can you start using these 10 ways of living restoratively in your own life?

❖ How would adding any of these ways of living restoratively change your life?

❖ Practice one of the 10 Restorative Habits listed above. Discuss, or make notes about, what happened. What did you learn?

MENTAL HEALTH CHECK-IN:

Take time to reflect on your overall mental health. Consider if you should talk to a professional. Examine your mental health for signs of depression and/or anxiety.

Do I need more help with my current mental health?

_____

What actions can I take to improve my mental health?

_____

Have I been withdrawing from life? If so, in what ways?

_____

Could I find help from a counselor?

_____

What local counseling services are available?

Who can I talk to about my current mental health?

_____

ACTION EIGHT:

CHALLENGE AND SUPPORT

Anytime you seek to change your attitudes, behaviors, or habits, you need to hold two forces in balance: the *challenges* you face to grow from the setback you've experienced, and the *support* you'll need to actually make the necessary changes. Create a chart for yourself, listing challenges for yourself in one column, and the support you'll need in a second column. Then share the chart with your Restorative Mentor, Restorative Small Group, or Online Restorative Community so they can help you experience the setback as an opportunity to grow.

List Challenges you're facing to overcome your recent setback.

For example: Schedule a meeting with someone who can help you sort out why you did what you did.

List Support you need so you can grow from your recent setback.

For example: Who can observe you so you don't mess up in this way again?

Think about the following questions. Write your responses if that's helpful:

> ## RESTORATIVE QUOTE
>
> *"Failure is not the end; rather it's a source of insight."*
>
> J.K. ROWLING

* List three challenges or fears I have overcome in my life. What support did I have during those times?

* Who could I meet with in the future to learn, grow, and challenge myself?

* How could meeting with these people on a regular basis improve my life?

* What are the four biggest distractions that keep me from reaching my goals?

* What possible rewards could I give myself for meeting the challenges I've listed?

Reflect about and then discuss with your Restorative Mentor, Restorative Small Group, or Online Restorative Community what has worked for you in overcoming past challenges.

_____

ACTION NINE:

SELF-CARE AND WELLNESS

Pick an area of wellness to focus on for a week. Choose what you think you need to work on, based on your own circumstances and resources. You will eventually examine each area in the "Your Individual Wellness" circle, so the order is up to you.

Restorative Questions for Experiencing Wellness

Physical well-being:

1. What is one thing I can start doing today to improve my physical well-being?

2. What are my short- and long-term physical well-being goals?

3. Where can I go to find help and support meeting my physical needs?

4. Who can I enlist to help and support me meet my physical needs?

5. What does my local community have to offer that can improve my physical well-being?

6. Do I have a good doctor who can give me an assessment of my current physical health? If I do, I will make an appointment for a thorough physical. If I don't, I'll ask for recommendations from trusted friends.

Intellectual well-being:

1. What can I do to take care of and stimulate my intellect and mind?

2. How am I stretching and developing my mind? What else can I do to challenge that growth?

3. What do I need to learn in order to do my work or school responsibilities better?

4. What books could I read to help me grow?

5. What resources are available to me to help me grow and achieve my intellectual goals?

6. Who can help and support me in my improvement of intellectual wellness?

Spiritual well-being:

1. What can I do to take care of my spirit?

2. What can I do to grow spiritually?

3. What can I read to grow spiritually?

4. What relationship(s) can I create or work on to support my spiritual growth?

5. Is there a place I can go to help me grow spiritually?

6. Who can help and support me with my spiritual growth?

Emotional well-being:

1. How am I doing emotionally? In what areas do I need to do some work?

2. Are there any behaviors that I need to address that relate to my emotional health?

3. What thoughts and self-talk do I need to address to improve my emotional health?

4. Who can I reach out to for help to support my emotional growth?

5. Do I need professional help? What resources are available in my community and online to help me emotionally?

6. How can I put my current worry into perspective?

When I am struggling or worried, I will ask myself if worrying provides me with more options or improves my situation in any way.

7. How can I use reason and logic to change the way I see my problems?

8. How can I release and share my emotions?

Social well-being:

1. What can I do to take care of my social well-being?

2. What do I need to do better in all my roles and relationships—with family, friends, people at school and at work, neighbors. . .?

3. What specific daily or weekly steps can I take to challenge myself socially?

4. Who can I talk to about my social well-being, share my concerns with, hold me accountable if I take risks, and support me in this whole area?

5. Are there any social relationships that I currently engage in that are unhealthy and have a negative impact on who I want to be?

6. How can I change or eliminate these relationships?

7. Are there any groups or clubs in my community I could benefit from joining?

8. Are there any service opportunities I could try?

Financial well-being:

1. What is my current financial situation?

2. Where do I want to be financially in the short-term?

3. Where do I want to be financially in the long-term?

4. What do I need to do to take care of my financial well-being?

5. What steps can I start taking to meet my goals and improve my financial situation?

6. How can I grow and learn more about finance? Who can help me do this?

7. Who can I talk to for help and support with my financial situation?

8. Are there any behaviors or habits that I can eliminate that will support my financial goals?

9. What resources and support are there in my community to help me better manage my finances?

10. Do I need professional help to meet my goals?

Environmental well-being (earth, nature, the planet):

1. How do I currently interact with the environment?

2. What areas of environmental stewardship, or care for the earth and living things, are important to me?

3. How do I contribute to the health of my surrounding environment?

4. What steps and actions could I take to improve my environment?

5. Are there any groups or organizations in my community I can join to better support my local environment?

6. Who can I talk with about environmental wellness?

Reflect and discuss with your Restorative Mentor, Restorative Small Group or Online Restorative Community what has worked for you in overcoming past challenges in this whole area.

———————————

ACTION TEN:

IDENTITY DEVELOPMENT: "BE YOU, UNAPOLOGETICALLY"

Reflect on your failure or setback experience and how it has changed you. Review your Restorative Story if you think that would be helpful. Don't judge. Don't censor. Just write down here what you think happened.

Now answer The Three Big Questions to see if anything has changed for you. Share your responses to the questions with your Restorative Mentor, Restorative Small Group, and/or Online Restorative Community.

Who am I?

Why am I here?

Where am I going?

❖ How did it feel to answer these questions?

❖ How confident are you in your answers?

❖ Would you have given different answers during other times in your life? If so, why?

❖ What would change your answers to these questions?

ACTION ELEVEN:

"TRUTH WITH LOVE"

Yes, you've seen this Action before. But because it is so useful, I want to make sure you haven't glided over it.

As you work with a Restorative Mentor or Restorative Small Group and become more comfortable discussing the ups and downs of your life, can you challenge yourself and find someone to give you honest feedback about your faults?

Caution: This might *not* be something you want to do while you're in the middle of a setback or failure. It is extremely difficult. Most people are very uncomfortable giving and receiving negative or critical feedback.

> **RESTORATIVE QUOTE**
>
> *"Who Dares, Wins."*
>
> BRITISH SPECIAL AIR SERVICE MOTTO

I recommend finding someone you trust and know well enough who will give you feedback that, in the end, will make you stronger. They are more likely to consent if you tell them specifically that you are asking for this, that you want and value their perspective, and that you are using this to make yourself better.

Tell them that you want them to offer what they see as your negative qualities, your blind spots, and how you are perceived by others.

If they say they can't think of any faults, ask them to think about it for a few days, and then meet somewhere where you're both comfortable to discuss the idea again. If they still say they can't think of any faults, ask someone else to do this with you.

You may want them to give you the feedback in small doses. One critical comment followed by two positive. This practice can change your life, but it can also be uncomfortable for both of you at first.

❖ List some people you can ask to give you the truth with love.

❖ Keep track of how you felt when you received the feedback you asked for.

❖ Note how you can use this feedback now and in the future.

❖ Reflect about how the meeting went and how you can continue to include this practice in your life.

❖ List other people who can give you critical feedback in other areas of your life.

———————————

MENTAL HEALTH CHECK-IN:

Yes, it's time to think about this again.

As you go through the process of rising from your setback and digging deeper into root causes, remember that it is important to know the limitations of the Restorative Process and when you may need more support. Recognizing and taking the steps to seek professional counseling is a sign of strength and courage. You need to continually take stock of your mental state and seek support if needed.

Am I depressed and/or anxious?

_____

Have I been withdrawing from life? If so, how?

Would my mentor or a trusted family member urge me to seek professional help? I will ask them to assist me in creating a plan to seek further help if needed.

ACTION TWELVE:

DEVELOPING A GROWTH MINDSET

A good resource to help you examine and make meaning of your setback is Mira Kirshenbaum's classic book *Everything Happens for a Reason*. She suggests that you explore what lesson(s) you've been taught by a failure. What positives can you take away from this experience? If this hadn't happened, what negative path might you have kept pursuing?

You might be thinking that this is going too far. That it's too much of a stretch to suggest that had I not failed, I might have missed out on something.

In science, experimenting—and then using the results of your experimenta-
tion—is how you discover what works. It is the same with your life. You need to
take calculated risks, experiment, and learn from
these experiences.

Having a Restorative Mentor or Small Group
with whom to share your struggles can help you
learn from other people's failures and apply them
to your own life. This practice can really acceler-
ate and magnify your growth. You are learning
from both your storms and others'. This can even
help prevent you from making the same mistakes
they did.

Ultimately, serious reflection and a growth
mindset can lead to a change in behavior. I feel
now like I do belong in my job. I am able to speak
up at meetings. I can take risks. And when I fail, it
does not mean that I'm a failure. It means I made
a mistake.

> ### RESTORATIVE QUOTE
>
> *"If you bring forth what is within you, what you bring forth will save you. If you do not bring forth what is within you, what you do not bring forth will destroy you."*
>
> GOSPEL OF THOMAS

Reframing failure

Individuals who believe their talents can be developed through hard work,
good strategies, and input from others, have a growth mindset. Your talents
aren't fixed; they can be developed and improved. The key is to accept that you
have not reached your full potential "yet."

Here's a simple way to understand this idea. Think about someone failing a
math test. When they get the failing grade, do they say, "I'm stupid and terrible
at math"? Or do they say, "That was tough. I haven't figured out how to do this
math yet"?

The key word with anything you are struggling with is "**yet**." As you have learned through the Restorative Process, you cannot undo failure, but you can change your self-talk after the failure.

Think about these questions, and then answer them:

❖ Which is my mindset? Fixed? Or growth?

❖ How exactly can I embrace a growth mindset and improve my overall response to life?

❖ How can a growth mindset help me when I struggle?

❖ How can a growth mindset help me with my self-talk?

❖ What am I currently struggling with or failing at? How can I reframe and describe my struggle using the growth mindset concept?

Vulnerability, or authentic sharing, is the key to having this work. Who can I share this with and be vulnerable with? My Restorative Mentor, Restorative Small Group, or Online Restorative Community?

How do I take what I learned about myself from this experience and become better?

ACTION THIRTEEN:

OVERCOMING YOUR BIGGEST STRUGGLE OR FEAR

Draw a picture of yourself doing this. Or write some notes about how that might look.

❖ What lesson(s) might this teach me?

❖ What experience might I gain from it?

❖ Why might it have needed to happen this way?

❖ What is one lesson I can take from my setback, failure, or storm to move forward in a positive way?

❖ Is there someone I can talk to who's had a similar experience and can help me make meaning from it?

> **RESTORATIVE QUOTE**
>
> *"Difficult roads often lead to beautiful destinations."*
>
> ZIG ZIGLAR

❖ How can I prevent this type of failure or setback in the future?

❖ Who can I share all of this thinking with? Who can help me
  brainstorm more ways to prevent this failure in the future?

———————————

ACTION FOURTEEN:

ENGAGEMENT

❖ Who can I help, or give back to, connected to my current struggle,
  failure, or setback?

❖ What group or cause have I often felt called to help or be involved
  with?

❖ What steps do I need to take to give back or serve others?

❖ What is one thing I can do right now to begin finding a group or cause
  to serve?

ACTION FIFTEEN:

STAGES OF CHANGE

(adapted from *Changing for Good: A Revolutionary Six-Stage Program for Overcoming Bad Habits and Moving Your Life*, by Prochaska & DiClemente)

Explore how motivated you are to change your behavior. Practice some of the techniques and processes that will help you to change (see pages 203-208). Reflect about them in your *Restorative Practices Journal*. Or discuss the subject with your Restorative Mentor, Restorative Small Group, or Online Restorative Community.

> ## RESTORATIVE QUOTE
>
> *"I'm just 'bout that action boss."*
>
> MARSHAWN LYNCH

1. Pre-Contemplation. Not seeing the problem. Denial.

2. Contemplation. Seeing the problem. Considering whether to act.

3. Preparation. Making concrete plans to act soon.

4. Action. Doing something to change.

5. Maintenance. Working to maintain change.

What is something I want to change about myself? Which stage of changing do I seem to be in? I will do my best to be honest with myself, based on where I currently am.

I want to remember that the change process is a cycle. So I might cycle through the stages many times before I actually commit to changing my behavior.

Doing the right thing at the right time

Explore these Experiences. After trying some of them, reflect on what you felt and observed.

❖ **Consciousness-Raising**: We all gain knowledge about ourselves and the nature of our behavior by becoming more self-aware. Because we may not realize the negative effects of our behavior, becoming more observant about it can lead to our making better decisions.

Reflect: How can I become more aware of the negative effects of my behavior? Who can I talk with who could help me see my blind spots related to my negative behavior?

❖ **Dramatic Relief:** We often become motivated to change when our emotions are aroused by a significant experience, which may be external or internal.

Reflect: How can I use my current moment of struggle or failure as a catalyst to start the process of change within myself? How can I use an event in my life to motivate me to change a negative behavior?

I want to reframe the way I think and talk about my failure, understanding it instead as a catalyst for change.

❖ **Self-Re-Evaluation**: I'm beginning to see that some of my current behavior conflicts with my personal values, life goals, and mission. How might I be different if I could change the way I act?

Reflect: I will try to journal about what it would look like if I conquered my negative behavior. I'll be as detailed as possible about how my life would change. I will also think of someone who I can share this vision with.

❖ **Environmental Re-Evaluation:** I am recognizing, too, that my behavior is having an effect on others and the environment. Some of my behavior is not only negatively affecting myself, but also things around me. I have to change.

Reflect: I will list all the people affected by my negative behavior. Who on the list might meet with me to discuss how it has affected them? I will journal about how I can use this to help motivate me to change.

❖ **Social Liberation:** I recognize that if I create some alternatives in my social world, that will encourage me to change my behavior. And help me maintain changes in my behavior.

Reflect: I will create a list of alternatives that will encourage me to change my behavior. I will brainstorm with others to develop my list. I will continue to evaluate these alternatives and how well I'm using them to change my behavior.

Behavioral changes I can make

❖ **Stimulus control:** I will avoid those places, people, and cues that tend to draw me into problem behavior. For example, places where alcohol and drugs are used.

Reflect: List all the cues that lead to your negative behavior. Create a plan to address or alter how each of these cues affects you.

❖ **Self-Liberate**: Start by believing in your ability to change. Act on that belief by making a commitment to behave differently. Think of small goals you can reach that lead to the bigger change you want to make.
   Reflect: Who are your current cheerleaders? Who can you enlist to be your cheerleaders along your change journey? Be sure to let them know how much you need and appreciate this type of support.

❖ **Counter-Conditioning**: Substitute healthy behaviors for unhealthy ones.
   Reflect: List all the healthy behaviors you can use to change your negative behaviors. Find someone who can help you brainstorm more healthy behaviors. Reflect and evaluate yourself regularly.

❖ **Reinforce good behavior**: How can you reward yourself for positive behavior changes you've made? What actual rewards would help you? Or are the positive consequences as a result of your changes enough?
   Reflect: List all of the positive consequences you've experienced while changing your behavior. Find other people who can help you recognize the positive changes. Continue to recognize and point out these positive changes to yourself.

❖ **Look for helping relationships**: Any of us who is attempting to make a change needs relationships that provide support, caring, and acceptance. They can be the most powerful help in your effort to change.

    Reflect: Create a list of people who can help you along your change journey. Develop a plan of how you will reach out to them and how they can support you. Continue to evaluate your support people, and change and adapt as needed.

❖ **Create a detailed, specific plan** to change your negative behavior. Be detailed. Include your short-term and long-term goals, the challenges you'll face, and the support you'll need along the way to make it a long-lasting change.

    Ask yourself, who can I share my change plan with who will hold me accountable?

    If you don't think you have a problem, how might you get an honest view of yourself so you know if you might need to make a change?

    Think back. Have you ever successfully changed an ingrained behavior on your own?

    How do you think you could move yourself to the next stage of the change process?

———————————————

ACTION SIXTEEN:

GRIT

Angela Duckworth defines grit as "perseverance and passion for long-term goals."

A quick way to introduce yourself to the concept of grit, and to see where your grit level stands, is to do a brief online assessment developed by Angela Duckworth. Go to: angeladuckworth.com/grit-scale

❖ What is your grit score?

❖ What did you learn about grit that you can apply to yourself and your Restorative Story?

❖ List what you are passionate about.

❖ Ask yourself, how could I turn my passions into a career or a lifelong pursuit?

❖ How can I use my grit—my passion and perseverance—when I encounter life's setbacks and failures in the future?

❖ As I think about my past, when did I show strong grit? When did I lack grit?

❖ What can I do to develop and grow my grit?

❖ Who do I know that has a high level of grit? Set up a meeting with them to ask them how they developed their grit.

ACTION SEVENTEEN:
SHARING MY RESTORATIVE STORY

When we share our stories, we take what we once kept in darkness and create a light so others can also find safety and comfort in knowing they're not alone.

Your story can help others feel understood. Sharing our authentic stories helps us all learn and grow together.

Are you ready to share your story beyond your Restorative Mentor or Restorative Small Group, as you discover others who are struggling with failure or setbacks? You can post your story, too, or make a video for your social media posts. But think first about *why* you might do that.

There is no one right way to do this—it's your story.

———————————

ACTION EIGHTEEN:

CREATING MY MISSION STATEMENT

Creating a Mission Statement can be one way to motivate you to achieve your goals and conquer your struggle(s). It can help to motivate your passion and persistence for doing day-to-day hard work.

In working with many people over the years, I've found that creating a simple one- or two-sentence Mission Statement—that you can easily memorize—can be extremely powerful.

See pages 106-107 to refresh your memory about how to prepare yourself to write your Mission Statement below.

These questions can help you shape what you want to say :

❖   Who are you here to serve?

❖   What is your purpose, or what do you feel called to do?

❖   What words inspire you?

Evaluate, change, add illustrations, and continue to adjust your Mission Statement as you refine or clarify who you mean to be.

ACTION NINETEEN:
MY VALUES

❖ What is important to you?

❖ What is essential to you?

❖ What values do you attempt to live up to on a regular basis?

ACTION TWENTY:
MY VISION

❖ What would your day look like if you were living out your vision and mission?

❖ What does your future look like if you are living your best life and being the person you say you want to be?

❖ What big, giant dream have you had for as long as you can remember? Write it down.

❖ Is there anything from your past that you miss doing?

❖ Think back. What has involved you so completely that when you stopped for just a minute, you realized time had flown by? Can recalling this help you find your way forward now? Is it a possible clue to a career or activity you might want to engage in?

How can the answers to these questions help you change your behavior, recover from your setback or failure, and help you down the path to becoming the person you say you want to be?

———————————

MENTAL HEALTH CHECK-IN

As you go through the process of rising from a setback and digging deeper into its root causes, be aware of the limitations of this process and when you may need more support. Recognizing and taking the steps to seek professional counseling is a sign of strength and courage. You need to continually think seriously about your mental state and seek support if you need it.

Do I sense any signs of depression and/or anxiety within myself?

_____

Have I been withdrawing from life? If so, in what ways?

Should I seek professional help?

_____

What is my plan to seek further help?

ACTION TWENTY-ONE:

MY GOALS

Goals are the paths of success you can take toward living your vision. What are some tangible outcomes that you want to accomplish along the way?

Be specific about your goals. Think beyond your current circumstances. A good standard for creating goals is SMART GOALS, developed by George Doran, Arthur Miller, and James Cunningham. SMART is an acronym standing for Specific, Measurable, Attainable, Realistic, and Timely.

❖ Long-Term Goals:

❖ Short-Term Goals:

More to consider: Here are a variety of questions to help you think and reflect more on who you want to be and what you want to accomplish:

❖   What resources or organizations have helped me rise stronger? How can I thank them?

❖   Who has supported me and helped me recover? How can I thank them?

❖   Who can I reach out to, to share my story and support my growth?

❖   Who can I reach out to, to introduce them to *The Restorative Practices Journal* and the Restorative Process?

❖   What else can I do to help others?

❖   Who can I serve? Where can I volunteer or serve others?

❖   Consider sharing the quotes and books you've collected with your Restorative Community.

*"The purpose of life is not to be happy. It is to be useful,
to be honorable, to be compassionate, to have it make
some difference that you have lived and lived well."*

RALPH WALDO EMERSON

ACTION TWENTY-TWO:

SELF-TALK REVISITED

Time to revisit your self-talk. This is lifelong work and, if practiced, can make a major difference in your growth. See Chapter 2, pages 35-57, to review what we know about self-talk. Start in. Update when you experience a major event, positive or negative.

Create columns for yourself with these titles in your Journal.

Date and time	Self-talk	Circumstances at the time	Reframed with encouraging affirmation

ACTION TWENTY-THREE:
ANGER AND FRUSTRATION

When we fail, we often become angry. Sometimes we start with directing our anger against others or against circumstances. It's okay to feel angry; it means you care and that you're not happy with failure. If you aren't angry, it likely means you're not bothered by this failure. Your anger, when channeled in the right direction, is powerful in helping you learn and grow from a setback. Anger used positively can lead to action and to making things as right as possible.

When a setback or failure makes you angry, answer these three questions so you can better understand what's happening:

❖ What am I angry about because of this setback?

❖ Who am I angry with because of this setback?

❖ Why am I angry with them?

"What if?" and "If only"

We all do this. It's human. We think back on the failures in our lives and review what we, or others, could have done differently to have prevented any of it from happening. (See pages 49-57 for a fuller description of this.)

It can be useful to examine and reflect on the "What if's" and "If only's" that come to your mind when thinking about your failure. If your reflecting includes considering how you might become more accountable to others, and how you might do better at controlling what you can control, you may be able to do things differently in the future. Which may help you prevent future failures.

But just dwelling on the "What if's" and "If only's" is not productive and does not promote accountability. "What if's" and "If only's" create a victim mentality—that things *happen* to you and you are not in control. If you are not in control, then why would you need to change and do things differently?

Name all the "What if's" or "If only's" you've thought of since experiencing your setback.

How can you think about this situation differently? How can you reframe the "What if's" to "What can I learn from this?" Or "This may have happened for a reason." Focus on what the lesson might be.

When you have a moment, or some extra energy, consider doing the following:

Restorative Quest: Pick one that you haven't done before from the 48 (see pages 236-246).

Restorative Trust-Building and Relationship-Building activity: Pick one that you haven't done before (see pages 247-254).

ACTION TWENTY-FOUR:

RESTORATIVE RESPONSES

Using a Restorative response involves applying what you have learned thus far, then going out into the world and doing your part to make things as right as possible. This is not only important when addressing your recent setback; it's also an important lifelong skill.

Look at the world. What might be your obligations in it? Make a list of the many roles you have in life. Then list all the obligations you have for those roles. Here is a list of some roles you may have. List obligations you likely have related to those roles:

* ❖ Partner/spouse:

* ❖ Family—my immediate family of origin:

* ❖ Family—anyone I consider family:

* ❖ Spiritual community or church:

* ❖ Employer:

* ❖ Co-workers:

* ❖ Children:

❖ Mentee:

❖ Mentor:

❖ Coach(es):

❖ Neighbors:

❖ Country:

❖ The World:

❖ Others:

ACTION TWENTY-FIVE:

8KQ

The university where I have served has come up with **Eight Key Questions** (**8KQ**) to put "ethical reasoning in action." I've listed them below. Or you can go to https://www.jmu.edu/ethicalreasoning/8-key-questions.shtml

Answer and reflect on them. They may help you face the ethical dimensions of a current situation you're in, expand your view, and see possibilities for restoration. Use these questions yourself—or with a group.

❖ **Fairness** — How can I act justly and equitably, while balancing the various legitimate interests that are involved in a particular situation that I'm part of?

❖ **Outcomes** — What possible actions achieve the best short- and long-term outcomes for me and all others?

❖ **Responsibilities** — Which duties and/or obligations of mine apply to this situation?

❖ **Character** — What actions can help me become my ideal self in this situation?

❖ **Liberty** — How do I show respect for personal freedom, autonomy, and consent for all involved? ("Consent" lets people choose and decide for themselves, and maintain control of themselves, their property, and their lives.)

❖ **Empathy** — How should I act if I really care about all involved?

❖ **Authority** — What do the legitimate authorities (for instance, experts, law, my religion/god) expect?

❖ **Rights** — What rights, if any (for example, innate, legal, social), apply?

ACTION TWENTY-SIX:

REVIEW, ASSESS YOUR PROGRESS, MAKE PLANS, TAKE ACTION

How have my answers to the Big Three Questions (below) changed since I began the Restorative Process?

❖ Who am I?

❖ Why am I here?

❖ Where am I going?

Reviewing your life Mission Statement

Is there anything you would change?

You have changed, and because you have chosen to make meaning and learn from this storm, you have changed for the better. Through the scars we develop from our failures and storms, we become changed persons. *The Restorative Practices Journal* is designed to help you periodically revisit your Mission Statement and vision and think about how a particular struggle fits into the big picture of your life. I hope you can see that you are not a failure. You are stronger and wiser—and more prepared for whatever comes next.

If you've just come through a setback, find out what you're thinking now by answering these additional questions:

❖ Why do I think this failure happened? Is there a higher purpose? What is the lesson for me, and maybe for others?

❖ How can I use this to grow stronger and wiser?

❖ How can I use this to help others learn from my experience?

Above and below are deep and powerful questions. It may be helpful to tackle them with someone else who has wisdom from experience, someone you trust, with whom you are able to be your authentic self.

❖ How do the choices you made that led to your setback relate to your Mission?

❖ How can the choices you make in the future reflect the person you say you want to be (your Mission)?

❖ What do you need to work on specifically? What does this work look like?

❖ Break this "work" down into steps and list them below. When can you start?

Reviewing your self-care

❖ What is my current living situation? How does it affect my self-care?

❖ What unhealthy things am I doing to cope with my recent setback?

❖ Did any of these negative habits contribute in any way to my setback?

❖ What am I going to do on a weekly basis to take care of myself?

Reviewing the Seven Areas of Wellness

(pages 121-129 and 186-194)

Assess your progress.

Review your Short-Term and Long-Term Goals (pages 214-216, if you recorded them in these pages).

❖ Who can I discuss my self-care habits with? Who will hold me accountable?

❖ What does it take for me to stop talking about what I want to do and actually make the necessary changes?

❖ Do I think I have a problem related to the behavior that resulted in my screw-up, failure, or setback?

❖ Have I acknowledged that I have a behavior that needs to change?

❖ Have I thought seriously about making changes to my existing negative behavior?

❖ Do I have a plan to change my behavior?

❖ What specific actions have I taken to change my behavior?

❖ Once I do start to change, what is my plan to check in, both with myself, and with someone I trust, so I maintain the gains I made?

❖ If I do lapse back, who can I ask for help?

❖ If I do lapse back, how will I hold myself accountable?

❖ How does my Mission Statement, and who I say I want to be, motivate me to take the day-to-day steps to change?

❖ How can I maintain my path towards changing this negative behavior?

❖ List here what motivates me:

❖ Who can I ask from my past to help determine what motivates me?
My parents, teachers, coaches, mentors, siblings, friends, and so on?

❖ What do I need to motivate myself to rise stronger from this setback?

❖ How shall I update my plan to change my behavior (see pages 206-208)?

MENTAL HEALTH CHECK-IN:

As you go through the process of rising from your setback and digging deeper into root causes, it is important to know the limitations of this process and when you may need more support. Recognizing and taking the steps to seek professional counseling is a sign of strength and courage. You need to continually take stock of your mental state and seek support if needed.

Are you depressed or anxious?

_____

Have you been withdrawing from life? If so how?

Would your Mentor or a trusted family member urge you to seek professional help?

_____

Ask them to assist you in creating a plan to seek further help.

ACTION TWENTY-SEVEN:
SERVING OTHERS AND GIVING BACK

❖ Who can I now mentor through *The Restorative Practices Journal*?

❖ Who do I know who is struggling, has recently failed, or is facing a setback—or who would simply benefit from these practices?

❖ What's the best way for me to reach out to them and invite them on this journey?

❖ Is there a group of people I could bring together to work through *The Restorative Practices Journal* as a team?

❖ What's the best way for me to reach out to them and invite them on this journey?

ACTION TWENTY-EIGHT— AND BEYOND:

ONGOING SELF-ASSESSMENT

I hope you realize that these practices are lifelong tools to help you overcome your screw-ups, make things right, rise stronger, and be prepared to face future storms.

Here is a self-assessment tool you can use to see where you are in your Restorative journey and what support you may need. It also will help you assess what challenges you need to take and how you can stretch yourself to become the person you say you want to be.

Journal on these questions. Reflect and discuss them with your Restorative Mentor, Restorative Small Group, or your Online Restorative Community.

❖ Do I have a growth mindset? When I face something challenging, do I say to myself, "I don't think I can do this," or "I can't do this *yet*"?

❖ Do I lean into the discomfort, the challenge, and the uncomfortable?

❖ Adversity: Do I embrace it or am I scared of it?

❖   Where is my focus? Have I stopped comparing myself to others endlessly? Have I learned to focus primarily on my own self-growth?

❖   Do I have a plan to change my negative behavior(s)?

❖   Reflect on my storytelling—both the story I tell about myself, and also my Restorative Story. How honest is my story of my recent setback?

❖   What view do I have of my future? How hopeful am I?

❖   Engagement: "The unexamined life is not worth living." Do I believe this and practice it?

❖   How can I use journaling as an ongoing tool to grow stronger?

❖   Books and quotes: What am I reading now? What quotes inspire me?

❖ Sense of belonging: What is my level of belonging in my current group? In what spaces do I feel like I belong? In what spaces do I feel uncomfortable?

❖ Challenge and Support (see all of Part 1, Chapter 7, especially pages 130-133): How do I embrace and use these concepts?

❖ Failure from a Restorative Justice perspective: Engagement, Harm, Needs, Obligations. How can I make right what's happened? Do I practice these 4 pillars of Restorative Justice? Do I practice them proactively?

❖ What is my current work ethic? Can I become a harder worker? In what areas of my life do I need to work harder?

❖ GRIT: Where am I on the GRIT scale? Have I grown in passion and perseverance (see pages 146, 209-210)?

❖ Who gives me Truth with Love? Who are my support people (see pages 98-101)?

❖ Do I have a Mission Statement (see pages 106-107, 141)? Do I use it as a
tool to make decisions and motivate my day-to-day behavior?

Continue your journey. Take these practices with you as you face new storms,
and continue to review and reflect on your mission, purpose, and who you are.

Mentor someone else through a storm they are facing, or start a small group
to work on the *Journal* together.

You are infinitely stronger and more capable than you realize. This *Journal* is
helping you bring out your best and become the person you want to be. Enjoy
life!

———————————

41 RESTORATIVE QUESTS
TO KEEP YOU IN PRACTICE!

Pick one or more of these 41 Quests to do between meetings with your
Restorative Mentor or Restorative Small Group, or between times of working
through *The Restorative Practices Journal* yourself. It can be helpful to do these
Quests with someone close to you, probably your Restorative Mentor or Restorative Small Group.

You can practice these Quests regularly so they become lifelong activities.
Their purpose is to help you examine your life and make meaning from your
experiences. Reflecting on the Quests with another person or a group will assist
you in making meaning and using the experience to grow stronger and wiser.
Have fun and embrace the journey!

1. "Truth with love"

This is a tough Quest, but if you make this a lifelong practice, it can really help you grow stronger. See hints on pages 92-94 and 96-97 ("Choosing a Mentor") about how to select a person who is wise, and who you trust, to meet with you. Ask them to come to the meeting prepared to give you feedback on the following questions, helping you see what you need to improve.

❖ How do I come across?

❖ What are my blind spots?

❖ What do you think I don't know but should?

❖ What are people saying about me that I don't know but could benefit by knowing?

These things are extremely difficult to hear and to tell. Encourage your buddy to be honest because you are asking for it. You may need to get just a little feedback at a time. Consider picking multiple people in your life to do this with so you get a variety of views and perspectives from different areas of your life. Finding trusted friends to tell you the truth with love is a worthwhile lifelong practice.

2.   Restorative thank you

Think of someone from your past who helped to make you who you are today. Write a letter, send an email, or meet with them, thanking them for helping you.

3.   Restorative apology

Identify someone from your past whom you should apologize to. Write them a note, send an email, or meet with them and apologize.

4.   Technology break

Take a day break or a weekend break from all of your screens. Turn off your phone and streaming devices. Give yourself a chance to break away from habits and try something new. The point is to examine yourself to see what role technology plays in your life.

5.   Learn to know your community by becoming involved

Try something new in your community. Look for an activity or relationship that strengthens one of your weakest self-care areas.

6.   Bookstore hunt

Go with your mentor or a friend to a local bookstore and pick out three books. See pages 107 and 147-148 for ideas about the kinds of books to choose.

7.   Creativity challenge

Paint or draw a picture. Show your creation to your mentor or a friend. Be ready to help them see what you've done.

8.   Pay it forward

Do a random act of kindness for a stranger. See page 202 for ideas.

9. Motivation playlist

Choose your top five or 10 motivational songs and make a playlist. Listen to it whenever you need motivation to face a struggle.

10. Picture/vision board

Create a picture, or gather magazine clippings or images for a picture board, representing your top five values, your vision, or Mission Statement.

11. Self-Talk journal

Keep track of your self-talk for a week. Write down all the things you find yourself thinking or saying to yourself. Share with your mentor. What are the themes? How would this talk make anyone feel about themselves? How can you change your self-talk?

12. Breathing techniques

Go online to find different breathing techniques and practice one technique every day for a week. A simple one to get you started is the box breath. Breathe in for five seconds through your nose and into your stomach, hold for five seconds, blow out from your mouth for five seconds, and hold for five seconds. Start by doing this for two minutes and work up to more. Talk with your mentor about how this makes you feel, and when are good moments to do this.

> **RESTORATIVE QUOTE**
>
> *"I breathe in my courage. I exhale my fear."*
>
> JONATHAN HUIE

13. Rise and shine ritual

Practice a morning ritual for a week. Perhaps try a new way of waking up or doing something productive as soon as you get awake. For example, start by stretching or going outside and sitting with nature. Could these become habits you can incorporate daily that would improve your life?

14. Self-Help book

Go to the library, or buy or download a self-help book related to something you want to work on. Read the book for 15 minutes every day. If you don't like the book, find another and start over. What benefits could you see from making this a life practice?

15. Workout challenge

Find an exercise that you've never done before and do it. Give it a good try. Do it with a friend or by yourself.

16. Meditate

Explore meditation online and then try it. Begin with a very short session.

17. For-me time

Set aside one hour during the upcoming week and do something for yourself. How could doing this help you in the future? How much time do you need? What all could you do during this time?

18. My space

Take some time to examine your space. It could be any room that's essentially yours, or your study space. Is this the type of space that makes you feel good, re-energized, and able to concentrate and study? What can you do to make your space help you be the person you say you want to be?

19. My people

Make a list of the people in your life. What is the first word that comes to mind for each one? What does each one bring to your life? Do they make you feel good or bad? Do they bring out the best in you or bring you down? Are they hurting or helping you be who you say you want to be? Which of them can be part of your support people?

Who is missing from your life? Who is your challenger? Who is your cheerleader? Who pushes you to do better?

20. Sleep

Do whatever you have to do to get at least eight hours of sleep a night for a week straight. How do you feel? How much sleep do you need to be your best version of yourself? How much sleep is too much for you? Experiment to find out the amount of sleep that works best for you.

21. Budget up

Keep track of everything you spend money on for a week. Examine the list. What are you surprised by? What can you cut out? How much money do you need to bring in to live the life you are living?

How do your purchases relate to your life mission, vision, and goals?

Think of your future and what your financial needs may or may not be.

22. Yum-yum challenge

Keep track of everything you eat for a week. What surprises you? How many calories did you consume on average in a day? Is there anything you should consider changing?

How does what you eat fit into your goals and mission in life?

23. Graduation card

Write a note to yourself about your anticipated graduation. Save this note and open it the morning of your graduation day. If you're not in school, think of another accomplishment that you're striving for and write a card to yourself to open on the day you reach it.

24. Surrounded by beauty

Make note of the beauty around you. Take a picture, draw a picture, or make a note of something you found beautiful this week.

25. New challenge

Find a new store or a new place in your community. Visit it and experience it with an open mind.

26. Old pictures

Go through some old pictures of yourself. What do you have to say to your old self? How have you grown mentally, emotionally, or both since you were that person in the picture?

27. Play time

Pick a game or a purposeless activity you like to do. Maybe a card game like UNO or rummy. The point is to do something just for fun without using screens and without thinking hard. Something that helps you to smile, laugh, and relax. Who would you have fun doing it with?

28. Your inner child

What activity, hobby, or pastime did you do as a child which you enjoyed so much that, before you knew it, an hour had flown by? Maybe it was doing puzzles, drawing, or Legos. Go back to your inner child and try doing it again.

29. Oh, NO

What can you say No to? Where can you take back some time in your life? Are there any activities or commitments you can say No to this week? Try saying No, and then decide what you'll do instead, based on your priorities.

30. Gratitude

List all the things you are grateful for. This is a great way to start or end your day. Practice this for a week. Reflect on how it makes you feel.

31. Negative to positive

Let this be your mantra for the week. Look for potential negative situations in your life and figure out a way to turn them into positives.

32. Two birds, one stone

Let this be your mantra and self-talk for another week. Look for opportunities to get two things done during the time you normally get one done. Or figure out how to create two successes out of one opportunity.

33. Through the Storm

Reflect and take a moment to look at how you survived a memorable or recent storm. Look at your present struggle. Find strength in the fact that you survived.

34. Restorative role models

Pick some people you know, or leaders from your past, who are examples of restorative leaders who have risen stronger from setbacks. Meet with them or talk with them about how they overcame their struggles. What can you learn from their hard times and their processes of recovery?

35. Storm chaser

How can you stretch yourself, take a risk, or do something beyond what you're usually comfortable doing this week?

36. Quotes

Collect quotes that inspire, push, or help you to rise stronger. Where can you post these quotes to help inspire you, create passion, or urge you to persist?

37. Books

Collect books that have helped you make meaning of your setbacks and failures.

38. Podcasts

Collect podcasts or online videos that inspire you or help support your Restorative Story.

39. Challenge and support

Look at your favorite book, movie, or moment in history and determine what the challenges were for a particular character. What supports did the character have? Make a list and take it to your next Restorative Mentor or Restorative Small Group meeting to talk about.

40. My place

Find a place in your community that relaxes you, inspires you, or makes you feel good about yourself. Go there a few times this week. How could finding and going to your own special place help you during the storms of your life?

41. Create your own Activities

Experiment, try new things, and reflect on how it went. Adapt accordingly.

———————————————

11 TRUST- AND RELATIONSHIP-BUILDING EXERCISES

Do these when you meet with your Restorative Mentor, Restorative Small Group, or Online Restorative Community. Adapt them based on your specific needs and circumstances. Find or create new activities to build trust and grow your relationship(s).

Preferences Exercise

Consider doing this with your Restorative friends. Feel free to add new questions or choices.

Circle the one you prefer:

Sneakers or boots	Eat in or eat out
Mountains or oceans	Trains or planes
Quiet or loud	Singing or dancing
Hot or cold	Past or future
Fall or spring	Sequels or prequels
Intuition or facts	Snow days or spring days
Gym workouts or outdoor workouts	Graduating or one more year
Save or spend	*Create your own and share*

Talk about why you feel as you do.

Eye Contact

Stand or sit facing your Restorative Mentor and maintain eye contact for 60 seconds. If you're in a Restorative Small Group, pair up to do the activity.

Talk about what it felt like to maintain eye contact. What can you learn from this Exercise?

Ratings

Do this with your Restorative Mentor, Restorative Small Group, or Online Restorative Community. Add new questions or choices if you want.

One is unimportant. Ten is extremely important. Circle the number that reflects what matters to you.

1. How important is it that your future life partner is on time?

2. How important is it that your future job gives you two weeks or more of time off a year?

3. How important is it that your future life partner is kind?

4. How important is it that you have over a 3.0 when you graduate from college?

① ② ③ ④ ⑤ ⑥ ⑦ ⑧ ⑨ ⑩

5. How important is it that you love your college major?

① ② ③ ④ ⑤ ⑥ ⑦ ⑧ ⑨ ⑩

6. How important is it that people see you as a person of integrity?

① ② ③ ④ ⑤ ⑥ ⑦ ⑧ ⑨ ⑩

7. How important is it that your future life partner is hard-working?

① ② ③ ④ ⑤ ⑥ ⑦ ⑧ ⑨ ⑩

8. How important is it that you have kids in the future?

① ② ③ ④ ⑤ ⑥ ⑦ ⑧ ⑨ ⑩

My Lists

Do this with your Restorative friends, adding any new lists that you want.

❖   List your top five books:

❖   List your top five movies:

❖   List your top five foods:

❖   List your five favorite teachers:

❖   List your top five destinations:

❖   List your top five songs:

❖   List your top five things to do:

Blindfold Exercise

Go with your Restorative Mentor or Restorative Small Group to a park or outdoor space. Have one person put on a blindfold while another leads them around outside, describing the place. Talk with each other about what it felt like to be blindfolded and what it felt like to be the leader. Switch roles and do the activity again. How does this experience relate to building trust and relationships? What is needed from both the leader and the led to make it work?

The 9 Questions

Talk about these with your Restorative Mentor, Restorative Small Group, or Online Restorative Community. Add more or different questions if you wish.

1. What was your most embarrassing moment in life?

2. Who is your one crazy friend who is always up for anything? What have you done together?

3. Who is your celebrity crush?

4. What is one thing you wish you had done in high school?

5. If you could have any job in the world, what would it be?

6. If you could live anywhere in the world, where would it be?

7. If you could sit and talk with one person, dead or alive, for 20 minutes, who would it be?

8. What is the first thing you would do if you won a million dollars?

9. What is the second thing you would do if you won a million dollars?

Shared Drawing

Choose a simple picture that someone could copy by drawing. But don't show it to your Restorative Mentor or your Restorative Small Group. Pair up with your mentor, or with another person in your Small Group. Stand back to back.

Give your partner a piece of paper and pencil. Describe the picture, so the other person can attempt to draw it using only your directions. When you've both finished, ask the draw-er to share the picture and show them the original. Talk about the importance of communication and sharing.

Deeper Questions

Talk about these with your Restorative friends. Add more questions as you're inspired to.

❖ What's the most interesting conspiracy theory you've heard of?

❖ What's one thing that most people don't know about you?

❖ What's your favorite vacation spot?

Two Truths and A Lie

Do this activity with your mentor. Or have each person in your Restorative group list two truths about themselves and one lie. Have the other person or group members ask questions to determine which are the truths and which is the lie. Ask everyone to guess which they think are the truths and which is the lie.

Together Logo

With your mentor or Small Group come up with a logo or team motto that represents you together. Where can you put this logo or motto when you meet? Can you create a centerpiece or symbol that represents this logo or motto?

Create or Find Your Own

Create your own, or find an existing trust- and relationship-building activity to do with your Restorative Mentor or Restorative Small Group.

Suggested Reading

◆ ◆ ◆

Baldwin, Betty Kilby and Phoebe Kilby. *Cousins: Connected Through Slavery, A Black Woman and a White Woman Discover Their Past—and Each Other*. Lancaster, PA: Walnut Street Books, 2021.

Frankl, Victor E. *Man's Search for Meaning*. Boston: Beacon Press, 2006.

Jones, Laurie Beth. *The Path: Creating Your Mission Statement for Work and for Life*. New York: Hyperion, 1998.

Kirshenbaum, Mira. *Everything Happens for a Reason: Finding the True Meaning of the Events in Our Lives*. New York: Harmony Books, 2004.

Ruiz, Don Miguel. *The Four Agreements: A Practical Guide to Personal Freedom (A Toltec Wisdom Book)*. San Rafael, CA: Amber-Allen Publishing, 2018.

Zehr, Howard. *The Little Book of Restorative Justice: Revised and Updated (Justice and Peacebuilding)*. New York: Good Books, 2015.

About the Author

◆ ◆ ◆

Josh Bacon, Ph.D., has taught and been an administrator at James Madison University, Harrisonburg, VA, where he served most recently as Dean of Students. He spent 20 years initiating programs in Restorative Justice at JMU, creating "Rebound," and bringing Restorative practices to the campus' discipline process. He has consulted with colleges around the country on Restorative Justice, with the City of Harrisonburg, VA, and with cases diverted from the criminal justice system.

Bacon played football in college, where he had his share of failures and setbacks. He enjoys sports, especially watching his daughters' games. He grew up in Chevy Chase, Maryland, and now lives with his wife and three daughters in Rockingham County, Virginia.